SESSIONS WITH EXODUS

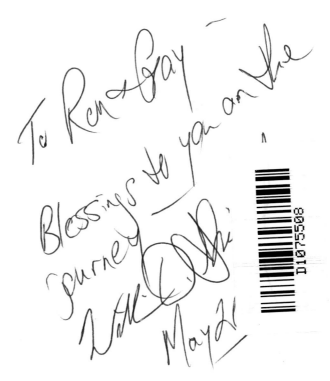

To Ron & Gay ~
Blessings to you on the
journey ~
Will ___
May 21

Smyth & Helwys Publishing, Inc.
6316 Peake Road
Macon, Georgia 31210-3960
1-800-747-3016
© 2020 by William D. Shiell

Library of Congress Cataloging-in-Publication Data

Names: Shiell, William David, 1972- author.
Title: Sessions with Exodus : questions god's children ask / by William D.
   Shiell.
Description: Macon, GA : Smyth & Helwys Publishing, 2020. | Includes
   bibliographical references.
Identifiers: LCCN 2020005634 (print) | LCCN 2020005635 (ebook) | ISBN
   9781641732390 (paperback) | ISBN 9781641732406 (ebook)
Subjects: LCSH: Bible. Exodus--Outlines, syllabi, etc. | Bible.
   Exodus--Examinations, questions, etc. | Bible. Exodus--Study and
   teaching--Baptists. | Passover--Christian observance.
Classification: LCC BS1245.55 .S55 2020 (print) | LCC BS1245.55 (ebook) |
   DDC 222/.120071--dc23
LC record available at https://lccn.loc.gov/2020005634
LC ebook record available at https://lccn.loc.gov/2020005635

Sessions *with*
Exodus

Questions *God's*
Children Ask

William D. Shiell

SMYTH&HELWYS
PUBLISHING, INCORPORATED • MACON, GEORGIA

Also by William D. Shiell

Acts
(Preaching the Word)

Ezekiel
(Annual Bible Study)

Sessions with Matthew: Becoming a Family of Faith

Reading Acts: The Lector and the Early Christian Audience

Delivering from Memory:
The Effect of Performance on the Early Christian Audience

To Drake
Because he asks me to tell him stories.

Contents

Preface

I have journeyed with the book of Exodus since I was a child in Sunday school. I have learned from Exodus as a seminarian, pastor, and now seminary president. At each stage along the journey, this drama has revealed something new to me about the journey of faith, the life of ministry, and the joys of serving the church. I am grateful to so many groups who have shaped these lessons. Three churches first heard these studies as sermons and provided helpful feedback along the way. Exodus was the narrative that shaped the journey of my churches as I trained people to take on leadership roles and preached sermons to cultivate generosity. My preaching students taught me how the journey from Egypt to the promised land is marked by long periods in the wilderness. Some of my students came from families who knew the agony of moving out of the "Egypt" of the Jim Crow South into the wilderness of Chicagoland. What was supposed to be a place of freedom turned into another world of racial injustice, redline housing, and mass incarceration. I have shared some of their insights in these studies, but I could not capture everything I have learned from my churches or students. Now as we face Covid-19, the book of Exodus has even greater significance for churches journeying through the wilderness.

Three commentators have guided my thinking from the beginning of this project: Carol Meyers, Walter Brueggemann, and Terence Fretheim. Their insights have helped me hear and see Exodus in new ways. This study is inspired by a question that Walter Brueggemann raised in the book *Reclaiming the Imagination*: "Will our grandchildren have faith?"[1] This probing question has been at the heart of every church I've served. Parents in the congregations have watched their adult children depart for churches that were younger, more conservative, or more liberal. Some of those adult children have left active church attendance altogether and only return for weddings or baby dedications. Members of traditional churches who once packed the pews four to five generations deep on Sunday morning now long for their grandchildren to come to Christmas Eve or Easter services at a minimum. These grandparents experience what is endemic to the church today. They live out their faith in a wilderness of sorts. They feel removed from their families who once attended church regularly, from a culture that once largely regarded Christianity at the center of society, and from a church that has often been unwilling to move from bondage into freedom. This book is written for those in the wilderness—everyone who longs for their grandchildren to have faith in God and wonder what the church is going to become.

To that end, I've taken the Passover scene in Exodus 12 as a template for character formation for people moving from bondage to wilderness. Just as it is written to encourage children and grand-children to ask questions around the Passover table (Exod 12:26-27), I'm assuming that Exodus continues to be passed down to the next generation orally and in writing at churches, family tables, and Bible studies today. Today's readers are part of that long line who have inherited this script and continue to read it aloud in conversation with congregations. Through preaching, drama, storytelling, and study, we pass faith along to the next generation. I grew up with and later pastored senior adults who were my grandparents in the faith. Today I serve a seminary that would not be here were it not for the sacrifices of previous generations. The questions that Exodus raises are the questions that we all ask along the journey. Exodus answers these questions with story, dialogue, mystery, and especially God's presence. In the end, the point of the story is to get us into a place where we can receive the presence of God for which our lives have longed.

I have divided these lessons into four parts in hopes that a family or congregation can read them together in light of the questions. The first part, "The Characters," identifies some famous and over-looked characters that God uses. Part 2 discusses "The Contest" for the hearts and lives of the people. I view the plagues or "fingers of God" as a performance to command the attention of the people that God wants. These events prepare Moses and the people to move to the wilderness. Part 3 explores the challenges and gifts during "The Journey" through the wilderness. We look at the changes Moses undergoes as a leader and at God's gift of the Law to constitute the Israelites as a people. We also look at the tests of dependence on God that are still relevant today. In part 4, we arrive at "The Destination"—a place in the wilderness where we are ready to encounter God's presence. We study how disobedience is part of the process we undergo as we design, follow, and construct a place for God to be with us.

I owe a debt of gratitude to so many people who have contributed to this project for more than eight years. Lorie Huff Matthews first transcribed my sermons into usable manuscripts. Dr. Claude Mariottini and Matt DeBall most recently offered feedback and editorial assistance in the final stages of the book. Many others read drafts along the way. I am so thankful for Keith Gammons, Leslie Andres, and the team at Smyth & Helwys for their patience with this project. I am especially grateful to my wife, Kelly, who for twenty-four years has lived this journey with me and has been a reminder to me of God's presence at each stage of the adventure.

My hope is that by studying the book of Exodus with wilderness eyes, we may see the place of wilderness at this time in our churches' lives as a place of God's presence (rather than punishment or absence). I hope this study raises more questions about our journey of faith, causes us to connect more deeply to other congregants ("called out" ones), and helps us see how our lives together can join the redemptive drama from slavery to deliverance. Because God is with us, we can journey courageously in the wilderness.

—June 2020

Note

1. Brueggemann, "Antidote to Amnesia," in *Reclaiming the Imagination: The Exodus as Paradigmatic for Preaching*, ed. David Fleer and David Bland (Nashville: Chalice Press, 2008), 8.

Part 1

The Characters

(Exodus 1:1–7:7)

Name the most significant characters in Israelite history. Who is the first that comes to mind? David, Samuel, and Moses probably jump out most quickly. However, the first two women mentioned in the book of Exodus are the real heroines of the story. As professionals in a marginalized community, these women initiate a plan that some thought even God had forgotten about. These women fear God more than any other power on earth and use a clever skill at their disposal to act on their beliefs.

As the story begins, we are drawn into a fascinating list of names that are probably familiar to the reader. The tribes of Israel are now safely in Egypt after God's provision through Joseph, the one who had been sold into slavery by his siblings. Their prosperity is quickly undermined by one whose name we never learn but who is only known as the "king" or "Pharaoh." This anonymous ruler knows neither the savior of the tribes, Joseph, nor the God behind the scenes, Yahweh. But he and God's people will know who this God is—not because of anything they do or what the tribal leadership provides but because of Hebrew women who work behind the scenes.

A study of Exodus can tend to focus on men such as Moses, Jethro, Pharaoh, Aaron, and Joshua, but women play a significant role, especially while the people are still in Egypt. The book opens with a list of the names of the twelve sons of Israel, signifying their tribal identity. Chapters 1–2 also include twelve women who will play a significant role in the drama. As Carol Meyers suggests, they are a "rhetorical analogue" to the men in the book.[1] We don't learn all of their names initially, but eventually we learn many of them as we read Exodus.

Shiphrah	Reuben
Puah	Simeon
Jochebed	Levi
Pharaoh's daughter and	Judah
maidservants	Issachar
Miriam	Zebulun
Zipporah and her six sisters	Benjamin
	Dan
	Naphtali
	Gad
	Asher

Unlike their male counterparts, these women form a mixed group. Some are Israelite (Shiphrah, Puah, Jochebed, Miriam). One is Egyptian (Pharaoh's daughter), and the rest are Midianites (Zipporah and her sisters). Some worship God; most do not. All are instruments God uses to shape, form, and prepare a people to be called out.

Exodus does not open with a mighty act of God or a charismatic leader guiding people out of a country. Exodus begins with a crisis of memory. The political leader Pharaoh does not remember Joseph, and the people think that their God has forgotten them. Behind the scenes, however, two midwives named Shiphrah and Puah have memories strong enough and a belief vibrant enough to take responsibility for the lives entrusted to them.

Fear Factors (1:1-9)

In order to understand the crisis of memory, we need to get a sense of the culture and climate of the Israelites as they lived in Egypt. Exodus 1–12 suggests they were stretched between the two poles of fear of God and fear of humans.

A LEGACY IN EGYPT

Let's review how they got here. The longer the Israelites remained in Egypt, the more they followed the command of Genesis 1:27, to be fruitful and multiply (Exod 1:7). They were in a territory they did not expect to occupy or possess. They had made the most of it, built on the legacy of Joseph and the fulfillment of a promise to Abraham. Wherever the people were, God was with them. This was part of God's plan, to do a work of creation, calling, and redemption.

Once enough generations had passed so that the pharaoh no longer remembered the legacy of Joseph, human fear drove many of the plans during a time of crisis. Pharaoh feared an ever-shrinking power base perpetuated by a prolific group of people who did not share the patriotic fervor of the native Egyptians.

As our story begins in Exodus, these migrant workers called the Israelites are now an integral part of the population. They are perceived as threats and treated as scapegoats by those afraid of losing power (1:8-9). The Egyptians fear a revolt in the population that could potentially overthrow them in battle. As a result, Pharaoh becomes increasingly brutal in his response; however, despite that brutality, the Israelites have persevered and been fruitful.

THE WAY OF LIFE IN EGYPT

After approximately 430 years, the Egyptian taskmasters depend on their labor force but grow deeply afraid of losing their power over them (1:11-14).

Nonetheless, behind the scenes, two professional women fear God rather than a human institution or ruler: the two midwives named Shiphrah and Puah (1:15). They do not accept the status quo of the Pharaoh's system. Their healthy "fear of the Lord" does not originate in threats of punishment but in awe, wonder, and reverence. This fear drives obedience despite the circumstances. Shiphrah and Puah behave shrewdly despite the great risk of opposing a powerful governing leader.[2]

Shrewd Strategies (1:10-22)

To address the population explosion and among the Israelites, the administration of the Egyptian king decides to "deal shrewdly" (1:10) with the people by embarking on a forced labor project. Like many oppressed groups throughout history, the Israelites are able to rise above Pharaoh's ruthlessness and continue to multiply. Consequently, he is left with one other terrorizing possibility: end life altogether through a program of selective infanticide. To implement it, however, requires the assistance of those he cannot control through his mighty empire. He turns to the midwives whose work has always been done privately, behind the curtain. The two women have a clever strategy of their own.

MIDWIVES IN THE ANCIENT WORLD

Before the days of obstetricians and gynecologists, in the ancient Near East only one person had a caretaking relationship with the mother before, during, and after birth. Through experience, magic, superstition, and prayers, midwives followed the moon and stars and brought life into the world. From the time prior to conception to a week after birth, life was a process. A baby was not considered "born" until three things happened:

1. The midwife prepared the birthing room, drove out the spectators, family, and others, and called on God to bless the delivery process.

2. The baby was delivered with the mother sitting on some kind of stool. Once the child passed through the birth canal, the midwife placed the child on the ground. Life comes from the earth, so this ritual connected the child back to the earth. Even today, we say, "From dust you were made, and to dust you shall return."

3. As the child began to breathe on their own, the midwife asked the parents to claim the child. If the mother wanted the child, she responded with a song or hymn stating that this was her child. If the birth mother was a surrogate, they waited for the adopting mother to call out in song, claiming the child. Once the child was claimed, the midwife placed salt on his or her skin to act as a preservative. The midwife determined if the child was healthy enough to live. If the child went unclaimed, or if there were problems, the midwife exposed the child in a field to wait for someone to claim the baby. After seven days, the baby was considered "born," a name was spoken and given to the child, and the child was claimed officially by the entire family.[3]

Our scientific world compartmentalizes fertility, conception, miscarriage, and birth into separate arenas. The midwife in the ancient world was involved at every stage of the process.

HIDDEN HEROES OF EXODUS

The Hebrew midwives are especially good at helping the women to be fruitful and multiply (1:10, 17). A pharaoh cannot stop life without them. But as Pharaoh noted, these women are not typical Egyptian clinicians. These are "Hebrews," a name possibly related to another ancient Near Eastern term, 'apīru, meaning "outcast, bandit, refugee, or fugitive." Whatever its origin, the epithet separates them from Egyptians. Their position outside Egyptian culture becomes their strength.[4]

These midwives fear God (1:17), and they refuse to kill Hebrew boys as ordered. Instead, they find a clever way to avoid the problem of Pharaoh. Because their work is secretive and because the administration cannot have access to the delivery room, Shiphrah and Puah save lives. As the Israelites become more prolific, Pharaoh's fear grows. He confronts them with a question, "Why have you done this and allowed the boys to live?" The midwives turn to another secret weapon. They disarm the "powers that be" not with a weapon of violence but with a whopper—a half-truth. "The Israelite women finish giving birth before we arrive," they say. They fail to tell the king about the God they truly respect.

Ironically, Pharaoh is more afraid of their work than he is of anything else. Using Egyptian and Hebrew customs to outwit the king, Shiphrah and Puah set the stage for God's continued work behind the scenes.

Let us pause our retelling of the story for a moment to address the structure of the narrative. Why would the book of Exodus open with a story about cunning women? The book discusses two themes. On the one hand, the book tells how God works behind and in front of the scenes of life to save God's people. We hear and read about several examples of people like Shiphrah and Puah who defy the odds and become exemplars of obedience. They are the hidden heroes of Exodus, obedient in the closed delivery rooms, cunning in the throne room, and so often left out of this famous story's retelling. They work behind the scenes without public recognition, much like the four African American women described in Margot Lee Shetterly's book *Hidden Figures* and later popularized in a movie of the same name.[5]

On the other hand, the story is a script to expose the power of the one whose oppression the Hebrews treated as the status quo. The book tells us how God shaped and prepared the people to be ready to be called out of Egypt. God needs to intervene in Pharaoh's heart to deliver the people, and God must convince the people to leave. The slaves are stuck in this condition. Pharaoh's tactics of fear, death, violence, and oppression need to be exposed. After more than 400 years, this kind of life starts to feel normal. Even if the conditions are oppressive, the Hebrew people cannot imagine another way to live. They have no idea these conditions they call "living" are poisoning their existence.

They need to understand that the pain of staying will be far greater than the difficulties associated with leaving. To stay is to die; to leave is to survive. Exodus teaches that God is in charge. People who are comfortably settled sometimes have to move. They have to get up and go on a journey. The process that the midwives begin reteaches who God is to them and exposes Pharaoh's strategy of death. God's people will not survive to tell their grandchildren this story without a whole new way and place to live.

Life with a Silent God

The opening chapter of Exodus provides a remarkable plot for conversations among parents and grandchildren about the life of faith. In this chapter, we meet two Hebrew women who use shrewd tactics in an environment of fear to save lives and expose the deathly intentions of Pharaoh.

Remarkably, God's voice is silent; God does not speak audibly until Exodus 3. God's silence, however, does not equal God's absence. God communicates through the behavior of people who are wise enough to obey. When the heavens seem to be shut, believers engage in several ways of living faithfully.

Tell the story of creation. God's story of creation and recreation is an ongoing process. It's not limited to Genesis 1 or 2. God is continually working to make all things new. In the case of Exodus, we will see this played out in birthing children (chapter 1), in cleansing the air, water, and land (chapters 7–11), and in saving the people (chapter 12). Each is an important part of the process of God's creative works: life, earth, and community.

When creation is viewed as a process rather than a singular event, we retell the story from a new perspective. Just as Genesis 1 tells the story of a people who were fruitful and multiplied, so the Israelites are fruitful and multiplying in a foreign land. They respond to oppression by continuing the work of creation. Their work and the work of the midwives is a story worth telling from their perspective.

Fear the Lord. There are two responses to any oppressing situation: panic or fear of the Lord. Most oppression is a result of the fear of others; a similar response only compounds the problem. Panic is the response of unbelievers. Believers respond by fearing the Lord. Knowing that God will pay attention to their suffering, the path of resistance in times of oppression is different. We join with other like-minded believers to live in light of the fear of God. This posture of awe, wonder, respect, and reverence demonstrates obedience. Two midwives can make a difference if they know what to look for and how to behave.

Take, for example, the role of Frodo in J. R. R. Tolkien's Lord of the Rings or of the children in C. S. Lewis's Chronicles of Narnia. These characters in these series believe that visible and invisible forces are at work in the world. Their role is to carry out their mission faithfully to each other and on behalf of their community and to leave the results to God. Eugene Peterson notes that there are some 138 mentions of fear of the Lord in the Bible, and this fear is cultivated by a lifestyle of awe, wonder, and beauty at God's design and work.[6]

As we tell the story of the midwives to our children and each other, we begin from the position of awe and respect, much as we would by reading a children's fairy tale. Exodus is not a fairy tale, but we begin the story with the same sort of wide-eyed wonder and imagination as when a parent reads a book to their child.

Take a risk. Shiphrah and Puah are positioned in such a way to take a managed risk to save the lives of others. This kind of resourcefulness, creativity, and shrewdness is not without precedent. God has a plan for the world, and part of the plan is to use the resourcefulness, creativity, ingenuity, and shrewdness of God's people to birth that plan in their daily affairs.

In the New Testament, Jesus describes the kingdom of God in the parable of a shrewd manager (Luke 16:1-13). In one of his most controversial statements, he likens the kingdom to a dishonest manager who is about to be fired from his job. Because he has no other skills, the manager writes off or decreases many of the debts owed to the master in order to secure friends who will hire him after he is terminated. The master commends the dishonest steward for his shrewdness. The parable suggests that Jesus values relationships over commerce. The currency of the kingdom of God is not merchandise, money, or material things. God places greater value on relationships with people. In the parable, by choosing to value the people, the dishonest manager demonstrates a kingdom-like quality.

The midwives value the lives of the Hebrews over the commands of a deadly Pharaoh. When forced to obey, they choose the path that brings life.

Do your job. Exodus is remembered for the legendary scenes of the burning bush, the public signs and wonders, the parting of the Red Sea, and the Ten Commandments. Just as significant as these scenes is the quiet work of two Hebrew midwives who simply do their jobs. While they work, they find an opportunity to live with fear of the Lord and, through obedience, save the lives of generations.

Let me share one example of a modern hidden figure. When Kathy Waller moved to Bolivia, she developed a unique ministry to Quechan Indian women in the village of Santa Cruz. These women, often victims of violent domestic abuse at the hands of drunk husbands, had precious few resources to purchase food for themselves or their families. Whatever money their husbands made was often spent on liquor and drugs. The women, who stayed home most of the day to care for their children, needed sustainable resources. Receiving handouts of food and clothes only perpetuated the problem. They needed dignity, so Kathy Waller and her team developed a business where women could come to Kathy's home, paint scarves, and sell the scarves to customers through mission organizations. The small industry provided guaranteed money for these women to eat, childcare for their children during the day, and dignity for them in the midst of oppression. Instead of remaining dependent on abusive and addicted spouses, these women found a way, through the clever resources of the Wallers, to live in a place surrounded by death. Some might call that a business, others a ministry, but from the perspective of Exodus it's simply being shrewd.

1. Who are the real heroes of Exodus? Where do these midwives rank?

_____

_____

_____

_____

_____

2. The midwives used a shrewd tactic and a half-truth to divert Pharaoh. When is it right (if ever) to shade the truth for the sake of life?

_____

_____

_____

_____

_____

3. How was the Israelite community being shaped by the events happening behind the scenes? What difference did it make to them for these midwives to carry out their strategy?

_____

_____

_____

_____

_____

4. When people are oppressed, what appropriate measures should believers take to intervene?

_____

_____

_____

_____

_____

5. Name some of the overlooked characters in your life. Who are the people behind the scenes whose faithfulness has shaped who you are today?

_____

_____

_____

_____

_____

6. What's the difference between human fear and fear of the Lord?

_____

_____

_____

_____

_____

7. Fear of God can often be interpreted as an excuse to threaten people into a relationship with God. How do we avoid using fear of the Lord as a scare tactic to motivate others wrongly?

_____

_____

_____

_____

_____

Notes

1. Carol Meyers, _Exodus_, New Cambridge Bible Commentary (Cambridge: Cambridge University, 2005), 37.

2. Eugene Peterson, _Christ Plays in Ten Thousand Places: A Conversation in Spiritual Theology_ (Grand Rapids: Eerdmans, 2004), 4.

3. Victor Matthews, _Social World of Ancient Israel, 1250–587 BCE_ (Peabody, MA: Hendrickson, 1993), 67–81.

4. Meyers, _Exodus_, 36.

5. Margot Lee Shetterly, _Hidden Figures: The American Dream and the Untold Story of the Black Women Mathematicians Who Helped Win the Space Race_ (New York: HarperCollins, 2016).

6. Peterson, _Christ Plays in Ten Thousand Places_, 44.

Moses: How Do We Remember Moses?

Exodus 2:1-25

Moses' origins, life, and motives escape public notice. He is hidden at birth (2:2-3), rescued from the Nile River, and trained in the palace of the pharaoh. Moses attempts to bury evidence of a murder and escapes like a fugitive. He cannot hide for long, nor are his secrets safe. Behind the scenes, God is at work. By the end of chapter 2, God not only finds Moses working for his father-in-law but also responds to the people's groans. For the first time in Exodus, God's name is mentioned, and God emerges from behind the scenes to respond to the groans of the Israelites.

Hidden at Birth (2:1-10)

Chapter 2 opens with irony and hope. One family from the tribe of Levi undermines Pharaoh's infanticide. The husband and wife are Levites, a preview of the role the Levites will play in the drama (Exod 35:25-35). As a Levite, their child will have a priestly role. Before he's used by God, he will survive Pharaoh's violence and his own self-sabotage.

When the child outgrows his protection, his family makes a papyrus basket for him. Much like the ark in Genesis 6 (the Hebrew word is the same), the basket becomes a place of refuge for the boy. They hide their child (2:2, 3) near the banks of the Nile River where infant Israelite boys are drowned to fulfill Pharaoh's order (1:22). The symbolism is rich here, as this child will one day lead people through water to safety.

Pharaoh's daughter secretively rescues the child. When she discovers him, instead of disclosing his ethnicity, she takes pity on him. The child's sister, watching from a distance, volunteers her mother to assist as a wet nurse.

Pharaoh's daughter names the boy "Moses." Even his name indicates that he is a child of two worlds. His name comes from an Egyptian root meaning "child of" and a Hebrew root meaning "from the water."[1] His name sounds almost Egyptian, like the pharaohs Thutmose and Ahmose. His name suggests what his role will be, a man with a foot in two worlds: Egyptian and Hebrew. He's also leading people from one land to another, from Egypt to the wilderness toward Canaan.

So much of God's work escapes the public eye from conception to salvation. Even Moses' parents' names, Amram and Jochebed, are veiled until 6:2. The author of Exodus protects their identity in this time of tension, irony, and hope.

Secret Life (2:11)

Once Moses survives infancy, he lives a secret existence, even hidden from the readers of Exodus. The narrator describes him as the boy drawn from the water with a resourceful sister and his mother as wet nurse, then simply indicates that Moses "grew up." We learn from Jewish and Christian traditions that the Egyptians shaped Moses' character (see Josephus, *Antiquities* 2.9.6-7; Acts 7:22; Heb 11:24). Acts compares Moses to Jesus. Just as Jesus grew in wisdom, stature, and favor with God and humanity, so did Moses. The Egyptians trained Moses, but God somehow used this curriculum to prepare Moses for leadership.

No matter what happens behind the scenes, Moses' education is incomplete. The Egyptian system gives him the competency to work but not the capacity to lead God's people. He has the position as a prince in the household of Pharaoh but not power from God. Moses has all the talent and none of the temperament. He knows all the facts of history yet possesses none of the context. When no one is thought to be watching, we discover his flaws.

A Buried Secret (2:11-15)

Unfortunately, Moses knows just enough about his history to be dangerous. He understands that he shares a bloodline with the people who are being oppressed (Exod 2:11). He sympathizes with them, and his anger bubbles out when he sees an Egyptian abuse his people. He attempts to right a wrong by killing the Egyptian. He tries to solve a problem and buries the consequences in the sand (2:12). The next day, he tries to solve a dispute between two of his own people, but his impertinence backfires. The Hebrews reveal that they know he killed the Egyptian.

The text is full of parallel stories and images from Genesis 6–8. Pharaoh uses the Nile to kill babies; Moses is rescued from the Nile. The basket is an ark of protection like the big boat was for Noah. The daughter of Pharaoh defies the pharaoh, attempting to become arbiter and judge. Just as Pharaoh said to the midwives, "Why have you done this?"(1:18), the Hebrews ask Moses, "Who made you a ruler and judge over us?" (2:14). Pharaoh attempts to do to Moses what Moses did to the Egyptian. Do you mean to kill me as you killed the Egyptian?" (v. 14). Moses replies, "Surely the thing is known" (v. 14). I've often wondered what or who this "thing" could be. Here are some possibilities:

1. Moses' crime. The "thing" could be the crime that Moses commits. He murders an Egyptian and attempts to hide the body.

2. Moses' motivations. Does Moses harbor in his heart the same anger, rage, and ambition that can become a toxic cocktail of pride, presumption, and hubris? When he's revealed, does he look more like a criminal? What does Moses see of himself as he stares at the sands of Egypt?

"The thing" may be none other than who Moses truly is. He's his own worst enemy. His greatest strength is his weakness. Everything that he has done to help and protect his people has made matters worse for himself. Moses attempts to play the pharaoh as a hotheaded judge and becomes a mirror image of the one he scorns.

Good intentions can go bad. Doing the right thing can be the wrong thing. Doing the wrong thing to make something right can be the wrong thing, especially when mixed with anger, privilege, pride, ambition, and youth.

As Gordon Davies suggests, Moses and we can never create our own missions in life. We can't pick a cause, join it, and solve it. A cause without a call of commission can be a source of arrogant impertinence. We risk sentencing ourselves to worse consequences.[2]

3. The people's uncertainty. The people are not yet ready for a leader like Moses. The Hebrews question him. Moses' methods are wrong, and the people are not prepared to leave under these terms.

As impetuous leaders often learn, those you attempt to serve do not always welcome a solution. Fixing a problem does not always motivate people to change. Solutions don't always lead to followers. We can still face rejection in the best of circumstances. Just as Moses needed to be prepared to lead the people out of bondage, the people needed to be prepared to follow.

God's people could not depart Egypt solely through their own willpower. They needed preparation and God's intervention. Similarly, a cluster cannot form a church simply of its own choosing. God must call them out. The Israelites needed to learn how to become the people God wanted them to be. In order for them to leave Egypt, Moses had to leave first.

Exiled Life (2:15-22)

Before Moses can lead the people from Egypt into the wilderness, he has to experience exile. In the land of Midian, he meets Jethro, a Midianite priest and shepherd who becomes his mentor. Jethro takes an angry, self-absorbed child of Egyptian privilege and helps him transform into someone who will have a role in shaping the people of God.

In verse 16, Moses asserts himself at a well and finds life. When the women are under attack, Moses confronts the problem without destroying the enemy. The man whose name means "from the water" gains respect from those who tried to "draw water" from the well. Jethro shows hospitality to Moses and offers his daughter Zipporah in marriage.

God Revealed (2:23-25)

When the king of Egypt dies, the Hebrews discover their problem cannot be solved with new leadership. The only way they can escape slavery is to turn to the God whose voice and presence they have not experienced in a long time. That's when God remembers them.

In Exodus, the act of "remembering" is not the same thing as overcoming absentmindedness. Memory here is the intentional and habitual recall of what God does with people who are ready to change. "Remembering" places something at the top of God's mind. This text provides a good list of what God does when God remembers.

Listens. "God heard their groaning" (v. 24). Just as Romans 8 says that the Spirit responds to creation's groans, so God responds to the people. God's work is an active, long-term response to the longings of God's people to be delivered from the place that holds them in bondage.

Recalls. "God remembered his covenant with Abraham, Isaac, and Jacob" (v. 24). To remember is to recall a vow that one made in the past and realize that now is the time to fulfill the commitment made to those people. In a marriage, vows specify the continual activity of remembering that affects obedience to one other. In these verses, one party has languished in Egypt; the other has waited. Now both have agreed to recommit to each other. God doesn't pick up where they left off. Instead, God returns to the beginning as if they were starting over.

Takes notice. "God looked upon the Israelites, and God took notice of them" (v. 25). Listening and remembering lead to an examination of the conditions and people that God is delivering. Remembering is an active pursuit. It reignites the memory bank of dreams and pursuits to say, "That is where we were. Now let's go together into the new future." We do the hard work to understand that we desperately need God. We know that we can't be the people we need to be until God intervenes. Then God remembers, and once God remembers, there is no turning back.

Remembering Moses and God

How do we remember Moses? As the fugitive from justice; the stammering, stuttering shepherd; the trained adopted son of Pharaoh; or the leader of God's people? We remember all of these traditions and more. Moses' complicated life speaks to the depth of his struggle and the lengths God will go to redeem people. God uses all of us, even the parts we would rather forget, as God calls his people. Moses was God's instrument even through the struggles. We can learn several lessons from this chapter that will guide us as we study the remainder of Exodus.

1. Without God's help, we can't be God's people. Moses' strategies and our initiatives fail without God's intervention. These events prepare Moses, the Israelites, and us to come to grips with our desperate need for God.

2. God operates and works in the least likely people and places. When we finally face what is going on inside us, God can reshape our lives. God remembers us as we remember that we need God.

3. Moses' conversion mirrors the people's preparation. Just as he was being readied for a desperate need to identify with God and God's people, so the people were getting ready to look to God for direction. For 400 years, we can assume that the people appealed to God to take care of them in Egypt. Presumably, they prayed for a

new pharaoh to fix the problems with the old pharaoh. God needs to prepare them to be the kind of people who can journey with God. A new king won't solve the problem, but a renewed commitment to God will.

4. Moses can't lead without having gone through pain. The only way to lead God's people is to experience exile. Christian leaders often identify with the statement, "I used to be a bad person, but I got over it." The biblical witness is that we never quite get over being sinners. We learn that God accepts and uses us as we are.

5. God can use outsiders to train people to follow God. Just look at the Egyptians and the Midianites. Both are formative in the life of Israel. We like to compartmentalize where God works, but no school has a foothold on God's work. God works everywhere and in every school environment—home, public, Christian, or parochial. God is always working. In Moses' case, he is educated by pagan polytheists like the Egyptians and by a Midianite shepherd named Jethro.

When the church gets involved in education, we have an even greater responsibility as God's people. If the Egyptians and the Midianites can point people to God's truth, imagine our responsibility to model the kind of life that is needed in today's world through the Christian example of service and sacrifice.

In one way or another, Christians are children of the water. Because we are baptized, we are "drawn out of the water." We have experienced a new birth of water and spirit. Christian formation explains and demonstrates this new identity.

Consider the role that public school educators have today. Many of them teach in environments where they are tested and evaluated based on the outcome of students who are a lot like Moses—brash and talented but with little character. God uses these teachers to form and change students at a particular time of their lives. Through their instruction and their compassion, they shape the lives of future generations. With eyes to see, we can view their commitment as a living testimony of God's work in secret places behind the scenes.

1. Most families have buried secrets that later come to light. How has God used these hidden things or people to show grace and mercy in your family?

_____

_____

_____

_____

_____

2. How does God use the Hebrews' conflict with the Egyptians to prepare the people to leave Egypt?

_____

_____

_____

_____

_____

3. God works in Egypt as much as in the wilderness. How does God use non-Christian systems today to accomplish his will? Who in public service today is shining God's light?

_____

_____

_____

_____

_____

Notes

1. Carol Meyers, *Exodus*, New Cambridge Bible Commentary (Cambridge: Cambridge University, 2005), 42.

2. Gordon Davies, *Israel in Egypt: Reading Exodus 1–2* (JSOTSupp 135; Sheffield: Sheffield Academic, 1992), 137–39.

God: Who Is Yahweh?

Focal Text: Exodus 3:1–4:17

In the opening chapters of Exodus, we meet women and a man who are part of God's plan to be present with his people. But God has yet to speak. For two chapters and 430 years, the people wait and groan. To give you a sense of this time frame, God is verbally silent for longer than the United States has been constituted. This time frame also explains why Exodus is so popular for exiled people. The book speaks to Israel's history before entering the promised land and relates well to hurting people who wait hundreds of years to be delivered.

When God does speak, he communicates through an unusual medium. God invites us to move closer, listen, dialogue, and follow God on the adventure, trusting in God's promise and presence.

Summons at Sinai (3:1-10)

The first word God speaks in Exodus comes from a *seneh* (Sinai): a bush that burns but is not consumed. The Hebrew name for the place where God calls Moses and where God gives the Ten Commandments is also the same word for the bush where God speaks. God communicates through fire to call the exiled prince to a new mission. In a pattern familiar in Scripture, God calls, summoning a person to a mission in order to accomplish God's purposes. In this case, God's call happens to someone who is not seeking to leave but who is carrying out his responsibilities on behalf of his father-in-law, Jethro, a pagan priest from Midian. Jethro will play an important role in the drama of leadership.

VOCATION AS A GOD DISCOVERY

In Scripture, the vocation, or calling, of a person is often tied to their occupation; occupation can be the place where we discover our vocation. But the experience of vocation is less about discovering yourself and more about discovering God. School (and often church) teaches us to focus on learning about ourselves—our temperaments, emotional patterns, and talents. We are trained to choose a major in college and a career path before we've done the character-building work of discovering what God summons us to do. Moses demonstrates that a call is less about learning who we are and more about discovering the One who calls us out of the bush. It's less about the choices we make related to education or career path and more about attentiveness to God's voice. We prepare to respond by tuning our ears to God's holy presence. Moses, like other ancient peoples, removes his sandals as a sign of respect and awe. He learns that the God he has heard about from his mother, the One who eventually settled his people in Egypt, now speaks directly to him.

GOD'S NONVERBAL WORK

God announces the plan for reconstituting his people and being present among them (3:7-10). Even though, until now, God has been verbally silent, he has been working on the people's behalf in unspoken ways. God's actions speak louder than words. In a series of declarations, we learn about a rescue operation that God undertakes on the people's behalf because their cries have reached him (v. 9). God declares,

1. "I have observed their misery."
2. "I have heard their cry."
3. "I know their sufferings."
4. "I have come down to deliver them."
5. "I will bring them to a land."
6. "I have seen the oppression."
7. "I will send you."

In some form, these seven verbs—*observed, heard, know, have come down, will bring, have seen, will send*—recur continually. When God appears to be silent or absent, he is working to recreate and renew his people. In the case of the Israelites, God's constant activity is the sign that God is not a passive observer to the plight of his people but is actively working on their behalf.

A Prayer Dialogue with God (3:11–4:17)

In response to God's engagement with him, Moses doubts. He questions whether or not the mission can be accomplished through him, fears rejection by the people, and wants someone else to confront Pharaoh in his place. This kind of dialogue appears to be more of an argument. Since Moses and God are communicating with each other, I describe this as a prayer argument or "prayer-guing." This is God's primary means of communication with Moses in Exodus (see Exod 17:1-7 and 32:25-35). In chapters 3 and 4, God responds to Moses' objections not by giving him more information about Moses' abilities but by disclosing God's own character, signs, and companionship. Moses' five objections can be summarized in this chart and are discussed in more detail below.

Category	Moses' Question/ Objection	God's Response
Personal Identity	Who am I? (3:11)	I will be with you, and as a sign you will bring the people back to worship here. (3:12)
God's Identity	Who are you? (3:13)	I AM WHO I AM. (3:14)
Audience Rejection	They won't believe/listen to me. (4:1)	Here are signs of staff, body, and water to prove it to them. (4:2-9)
Unable	I'm not a good speaker. (4:10)	I will be with your mouth and teach you what to speak. (4:12)
Unwilling	Send someone else. (4:13)	Aaron will go with you and help you. (4:14-16)

1. Personal Identity. Moses' first objection to God's call is personal. He doubts his own identity and his ability to lead the people (3:11). God responds by offering his presence, promising to accompany Moses to Egypt and back to the mountain with the people to worship God (3:12). God shows Moses that the only way to grow in self-awareness and self-confidence is to follow a God who is beyond ourselves. To see where God works, Moses must do what God wants. Obedience to the call changes the individual.

2. God's Identity. Moses raises a second objection. He assumes the people will question him if he does not name the God who sends him (3:13). God responds with a statement that describes past, present, and future possibilities. With the name "I AM WHO I AM," God identifies himself to Moses with the name "Present who creates Presence" or "God is who God is and God will be who God will be." God is present with the people and is open to the possibilities for the future. To give Moses even greater clarity, God instructs him to tell the people that this is the same God their ancestors Abraham, Isaac, and Jacob worshiped in the past. God's name reveals God's mission—to be present among the people in the present. God wants to form a people who will worship him and will create a place for him to be experienced in the midst of their worship.

God gives Moses his first speech, reiterates God's response to the people's groans, outlines the departure, and previews the Egyptians' response (3:16-22). The speech is remarkable on several fronts. The journey into the wilderness to make a sacrifice was intended to last three days. Even though the king of Egypt will reject the message from God, God plans a series of performances that will demonstrate his power. The Egyptian people will also send their valuables with the Israelites on their journey.

3. Audience Rejection. Third, Moses is afraid the Israelites will reject him (4:1). He recognizes that a leader needs the people to listen, and he doubts the people will believe that the Lord has appeared to Moses. To prepare him, God chooses to use common tools at Moses' disposal to conduct signs indicating that God's presence is with him—a staff, Moses' body, and water (4:2-9). Each one signals God's commitment to the task and marks another step of surrender for Moses on the journey.

To overcome fear of the audience's response, God equips Moses to trust in God's performative power. He shows Moses how to use the tools at his disposal to display God's presence. In much the same way that a conductor rehearses prior to a concert, Moses rehearses his part. By gaining the support of the people, Moses will have the confidence to appear before the king of Egypt using these three tools.

Staff: The staff symbolizes Moses' former occupation as a shepherd. He once fought off predators from Jethro's flocks. God now uses the same instrument for a different purpose. Moses must first let go of the staff, risk injury by picking up a deadly viper, and then use the snake/staff for a new purpose. By throwing down the staff, he sees that the object that was the symbol of his old life can also kill him when not used properly. What he grasps too tightly can lead to death. By throwing it down, Moses sees that God can take what eats us alive and make something good out of it—another instrument in God's hands.

Body: The hand signifies Moses' control over his life through which God uses his body as a vessel to demonstrate God's power in and through Moses. He turns his hand leprous—an incurable skin disease that forced people to be quarantined—and then returns the hand to its whole state. God has power over Moses' body when Moses surrenders to the Lord.

Water: The third sign will be water from the Nile. God will demonstrate his power over creation. This instruction previews one of the signs that God uses in his public performance before the pharaoh and the people in Exodus 7:14-24.

4. *Unable.* Moses' fourth objection reveals a condition that Moses describes as "slow of speech and slow of tongue" (4:10). People have traditionally assumed that this means Moses stuttered. In light of the way speech is viewed in the ancient world, it's also possible that Moses had stage fright. Ancient people perceived speech differently. Today, we think of the mind as the container of thoughts that eventually flows out of the mouth. Ancient people assumed that words remained in the mouth before they were spoken, so the mouth and the tongue functioned differently (Apuleius, *Apol.* 7; Plutarch, *Garr.* 503C). The mouth worked like a file system, holding words until the tongue and mind decided prudently what to say. The mouth was also a portal of character. If too much came forth from the mouth too quickly, ancient people assumed the person was a fool. Talking too much or impudently was a sign of foolishness. God could empower someone with divine wisdom even without the ability to speak eloquently. The tongue and lips then articulated what was held in the mouth.

God responds by reassuring Moses that he will "be with your mouth and teach you what you are to speak" (4:12). Through instruction, God gives Moses the words to say, placing them in his mouth so that he will be prepared to articulate the words. He will practice them before he speaks publicly.[1]

Moses' stage fright (not stammering) and God's response might explain why Moses wants God to send someone else. He realizes that if God places words in his mouth, he will then know what to say and be forced to speak publicly. That is, if the words are already there, Moses has no excuse not to obey God.

5. Unwilling. Moses' fifth objection is a demand for someone else entirely (4:13). God answers like an angry parent of a teenager. Moses provokes God, and God's default response is often burning frustration out of God's commitment to them. God changes Moses' role from spokesman to medium. Aaron will be the "director of communications" for the mission, but he will only speak what is spoken to him (4:14-16). In verse 16, God says Moses will be as God for Aaron, and Aaron will be the chief spokesman.

This tradition of the leader-spokesman has a long-standing history in ancient Israel. Jesus later trained the disciples to prepare for their appearance before "kings and synagogues" the same way God prepped Moses. In Luke 21:15, Jesus gives his disciples a "mouth [or words] and wisdom" that no one will be able to contradict. Like Moses and Aaron standing before the king of Egypt, Jesus empowers the disciples to improvise in the midst of their fear. Instead of rehearsing beforehand what to say, they trust that God will be with them the way God was with Moses before Pharaoh.[2]

Living the Questions

In *Letters to a Young Poet*, Rainer Maria Rilke wrote,

> Have patience with everything that remains unsolved in your heart. Try to love the *questions themselves*, like locked rooms and like books that are written in a foreign tongue. Do not now seek the answers which cannot be given you because you would not be able to live them. It is a question of experiencing everything. Live the question now.[3]

Moses' questions and God's rehearsal indicate how the Israelites will "live the questions" throughout the book of Exodus. There is no way to get through the wilderness in God's presence without living into the questions. Moses is just as insecure about himself and his status with the people as he is with God. What do we learn when we use questions as a portal into a life of obedience?

1. God is active in the silence. The perception of God's absence does not equal God's inactivity. As we learned in Exodus 3:7-10, God actively engages in seven redemptive actions behind the scenes. While we groan, God works. God is also not waiting for our groans in order to begin working. He is not a genie responding because of our prayers. God is actively engaged with his people and responsive to their needs because he is God.

2. Arguing with God leads to greater self-understanding and a clearer direction forward. God reveals his character as Moses argues against carrying out God's wishes. The excuses of Moses become levers that open the doorway of obedience. The more Moses argues, the more he obeys. If you want to obey, start disagreeing with God. He would rather hear us say "no" than "I don't care" or "I'm worshiping another god." "No" is at least a reaction; we've had to think about it. Every debate invites Moses even closer to the real hero. The hero of the story is God.

3. On the transformational journey, the objects we have become instruments in God's performance. Moses rehearses a creation pageant that God produces for the people. The pathway through the wilderness is guided by the ways God uses the tangible possessions at his disposal to reveal who God is and what God wants to do. There is no deliverance of the people without the redemptive performance in front of the king. In a similar way, the objects that we possess can be used as God's instruments if we surrender them. By allowing God to use our tools as instruments, we trust God through the wilderness. The objects that secure our past to reveal God's character in the future. God often uses what we already have to do God's work in the present and future. The challenge is to treat these objects as vessels for God's use. In order to see the new thing that God is doing, we need to surrender the objects that remind us of the past and give us a sense of security in the present. For Moses, it was his staff and his hands. For us, laying down the objects or people that have a hold on us releases them into God's use.

4. God sends people to help us. Aaron was already on the way to meet with Moses before Moses pleads with God to choose someone else to carry out God's plan. God commissions Aaron to a different task than was originally intended, but God never wants Moses to go back to Egypt alone.

5. God plans to improvise. Scripted speeches, although valuable, are not nearly as important as divine empowerment. When we rehearse what we know, God gives us the words to say. Moses learns to improvise what to say based on his preparation with God. Time spent practicing with the tools becomes an important pathway to preparation before the pharaoh.

Even the route of deliverance is unrehearsed. No matter which direction we go, the most important way is the way that leads back to worshiping God. We trust in God and surrender the future to God, knowing that God will lead us to a mountain to worship and fellowship. We must be open and honest enough to say that this God is living and active and can change his mind if God chooses.

God invites Moses into a new reality. Moses can't solve the bondage, heartache, and hurts of life. But God can address them by helping Moses know what to think about himself, what to do with the Israelites, and how to communicate with them. We should seek knowledge of the One who said, "I'm the one who has been there for your grandfathers, but you can't predict how I'm going to do this. I am the one you are going to worship, but how you will get to that point will be up to me."

6. Calling is best discovered by learning more about God. We live in a society that encourages us to make choices about identity, life goals, college majors, hobbies, and sports early in life. Consider these quotes from popular writers in literature:

• William Ernest Henley: "I am the master of my fate, I am the captain of my soul"[4]

• Robert Frost: "Two roads diverged, and I took the one less traveled by."[5]

• Rudyard Kipling: "If you can keep your head when all about you / Are losing theirs and blaming it on you; / If you can trust yourself when all men doubt you, then you'll be a man my son."[6]

At the core of each statement is a theme we teach our children: you can trust your instincts. As you make the best choices in life, you will choose a path for yourself. You are the best one to decide what to do.

The Exodus journey reveals, however, that we can't trust our own judgment. Moses' life illustrates that we have deep problems, and eventually they come bubbling out. The Exodus journey informs us that even in a self-imposed exile (Exod 2:11-15), God finds us. God invites us on a theological discovery that leads us to a greater understanding of ourselves. By looking upward and outward through prayer-guing, obedience, and sacrifice, we are best able to understand what God wants to do with us. The pursuit of God does not diminish the importance of free will in the process. As we have already discovered, God incorporates Moses' resistance and demands in their exchange. God expects that we will be making choices. The first step, and the most important part of the process, is to journey into the mysterious unknown with God, learning more about God. As we grow, God speaks to us too. Consider how the questions Moses asked God relate to your journey:

1. What do you hold in your hand?
2. What about your brother/sister/friend/colleague?
3. Who gives speech to mortals? Who makes them mute or deaf, seeing or blind? Is it not I, the Lord?

By remaining in the dialogue with God, we learn to obey. We obey even when we can't see the full picture. We walk blindly by faith.

1. Look back on a time in your life when you experienced God's silence. What was God doing on your behalf that you eventually learned further down the road of your life journey?

_____

_____

_____

_____

_____

2. Rather than passively accepting his calling from God, Moses prays and argues with God, resisting God's efforts to call Moses. God works with that resistance. What are some circumstances in your life that you simply accept as the way things are? How might God be wanting you to talk with him about these instead of accepting them?

_____

_____

_____

_____

_____

3. How does learning more about God reveal more about yourself?

_____

_____

_____

_____

_____

4. Who or what do you hold in your hand today that needs to be surrendered so that God can use it as his instrument?

_____

_____

_____

_____

_____

Notes

1. William D. Shiell, "'I Will Give You a Mouth and Wisdom': Prudent Speech in Luke 21:15," *Review and Expositor* 112/4 (2015): 614.

2. Shiell, "Mouth and Wisdom," 615.

3. Rainer Maria Rilke, *Letters to a Young Poet*, trans. M. D. Herter Norton, rev. ed. (New York: Norton, 1962), 35.

4. W. E. Henley, "Invictus," in *Invictus: Selected Poems and Prose of W. E. Henley*, edited by John Howlett (Portland, OR: Sussex Academic Press, 2018), 59.

5. Robert Frost, "The Road Not Taken," in *The Road Not Taken, Birches, and Other Poems* (Claremont, CA: Coyote Canyon Press, 2010), 9.

6. Rudyard Kipling, "If," in *Kipling Poems*, Everyman's Library (New York: Alfred Knopf, 2007), 170.

Zipporah:
Who Married Moses?

Focal Text: Exodus 4:18-31

What kind of a God will Yahweh be? Each chapter of Exodus discloses another aspect of God's character. In one of the most enigmatic sections of the book of Exodus, God demonstrates his relentlessness through the actions and interventions of Moses' wife Zipporah. (See the verses about their marriage and son in Exodus 2:21-22.) The dramatic scene is like an intense dress rehearsal for an eventual performance in front of Pharaoh in chapters 7–14. On the journey to Egypt, God prepares Moses for his role as a messenger and uses Zipporah, Moses, and Aaron to demonstrate that God cannot be controlled. We learn to follow the example of Zipporah, who respects God and protects Moses.

Return to Egypt (4:18-20)

When we last heard from Moses the messenger, God confronted him with the choice of whether to obey God. Moses has learned enough about God to know that this is not just some person. This is the ultimate, all-powerful God. He has also learned enough to know that serving this God could be a dangerous enterprise. This God speaks through a bush that ignites but is not fully consumed. God negotiates and compromises. No matter which excuses Moses offers, God is willing to counter the offer. God uses shrewd people like the midwives in 1:18 and even deceitful people like Moses. God can see through hypocrisy, and Moses is no exception.

As the scene opens, Moses attempts to take the initiative. He wants a family reunion. Appearing at the tent of his father-in-law Jethro, he says, "Let me go back to Egypt to see if any of my people are still alive" (4:18). God, however, is the one who coordinates Moses' travel schedule. He forestalls Moses until those seeking to kill him are gone. (We will see the irony of this in just a few verses.) The Lord ultimately gives him permission, saying, "Go back to Egypt, for all the men who wanted to kill you are dead" (4:19).

The Gospel of Matthew traces a similar journey when Joseph and Mary return from Egypt. They follow a course much like Moses and Zipporah's but in reverse. God speaks in a dream to Joseph; without argument, Joseph places his wife and son on a donkey and goes to Nazareth.

God speaks to both fathers. God assaults Moses but protects Joseph the entire way home. Consider the comparisons:

Exodus 4:18-20	Matthew 2:19-23
Moses, Zipporah, Sons	Joseph, Mary, Jesus
Return to Egypt	Depart from Egypt
Deaths of the ones seeking to kill Moses	Death of the king seeking to kill Jesus
Placed wife and sons on a donkey	Took the child and his mother to Nazareth
Heard message directly from God	Heard message directly from God
Attacked by God	Threatened by Archelaus
Rescued by Zipporah	Took refuge in Nazareth

Rehearsal for a Pharaoh (4:21-23)

On the way to Egypt, God explains the plan. Moses will stage a rigged magic show in Pharaoh's performance hall. Initially, the wonders and tricks up Moses' sleeve are designed to gain an audience with Pharaoh. After performing them for others, he will get his desired audience so he can confront the power that enslaves his people.

SCRIPT

God explains the script that Moses will follow (4:21-23). Moses will use magical signs and wonders that God has taught him to perform. The show is rigged in two ways. (1) The tricks are not for Pharaoh, because Moses and God know that the judge of the show will reject the performance. (2) Moses will use magical signs to show the Hebrews that they are the firstborn children of God (4:23).

The signs are gestures of God's character toward the people. Moses will certainly attempt to get the Egyptians to believe, as futile as the attempt may be. Just as important as Pharaoh's response is the people's trust. In order to leave Egypt, the Hebrews need to trust God and God's messenger Moses. The signs are designed for the Hebrews. The wonders demonstrate that this God is worth following. They will have to be willing to journey to a place where there is no water and to a land that none of them have seen. Moses uses the signs to demonstrate his reliability amid the uncertainty.

AUDIENCE

God explains that the pharaoh, the audience and judge of the performance, will reject Moses' demand—not because of Moses' performance but because something else happens to the pharaoh that is beyond his control. Just as Moses does not return to Egypt without God's direction, so Pharaoh is unable to judge a performance without God's influence. Without Pharaoh even recognizing it, God will "harden his heart" (4:21).

Here we get the first encounter with the theme of obduracy, also known as hardening of the heart or being stiff-necked, that runs throughout Exodus and is featured prominently in the deliverance. God says to Moses, "While you're on Pharaoh's stage doing your thing, I'll be working behind the curtain of Pharaoh's heart. While you perform the signs and wonders, I will harden the heart of the judge so he won't let your people leave." As the cycle of signs plays out, this proves to be the case most of the time. At other times, Pharaoh rejects God's message on his own initiative. And at still other times, the cause is unknown. The following table illustrates the references to obduracy in Exodus and the agent who causes it.

Causes of Obduracy in Exodus 4:21–32:7

Text	Agent
4:21	God
7:3	God
7:13	Unknown
7:22	Unknown
8:15	Pharaoh
8:32	Pharaoh
9:7	Unknown
9:12	God
9:34	Pharaoh
10:1	God
10:20	God
10:27	God
11:10	God
14:4-8	God
14:17	God
32:7	Israel

Consider how the idea of hardening one's heart functions in the book of Exodus. Obduracy works like gristle in your mouth after chewing a bad piece of steak. The more you chew, the less it digests. The longer it takes, the harder it gets. The heart of Pharaoh gets harder the longer the challenge continues.

The theme of obduracy suggests that God reaches out to Egyptians and Hebrews through a series of actions designed to evoke a response from them. Obduracy toughens the people of God to make them more resilient for the work and difficulty ahead. Instead of viewing the obduracy of Pharaoh as God's capricious punishment of the Egyptians, we can view obduracy as one of the ways God tries to get Pharaoh's attention.

We'll never know if Pharaoh could have changed or if his son could have been spared. That's the tragedy of this story. Some things, especially the death of a child, cause unresolved pain. By the end of the exchange, Pharaoh loses his firstborn son. In my view, the God of the Hebrews wants to be the God of Pharaoh too. But through a combination of God's choices and Pharaoh's decisions, Pharaoh never fully changes.

RATIONALE

With the confidence of knowing how Pharaoh will respond, God prepares Moses to communicate one more message (4:22-23): Israel is God's firstborn son. Moses suggests to Pharaoh that he is holding hostage the children of the all-powerful God. Moses elevates Israel's status. Pharaoh has never imagined that anyone other than an Egyptian could have the status of a child of God. But to hold God's children captive is to provoke a reaction from God.

Rescue by Zipporah (4:24-26)

With the message scripted and the messenger rehearsed, the story takes an odd and remarkable twist. God, Moses, and Moses' family stop at a lodging place. While there, God assaults Moses and attempts to kill his own messenger. Recall that God has delayed Moses' travel to avoid the people who plot against Moses. While scholars offer a variety of interpretations for this incident, the only one that makes sense to me is that Moses still has not fully committed to the task ahead.

Even with the script in hand, Moses wants a nice, safe God that he can use for a few tricks to bail him out. Just as God tests Pharaoh to toughen him up, so God tests his own prophet. Moses falls into the line of many other characters in the Pentateuch (the books of Genesis–Deuteronomy) who can't control or tame the actions of the one true God. They place their lives into the hands of God in order to follow him. Abraham endures the test over the sacrifice of his son. Noah watches as his entire world is destroyed by a flood while only his family is rescued. Jacob wrestles with the angel of God at Jabbok.

Moses' story is slightly different. He survives not because he endures on his own but because his wife intervenes. Zipporah appears in the book of Exodus three times, and this is the only time she speaks. We know little about her. She is a pagan Midianite. Her father is likely an astrologer. She does not yet worship this God. Until Moses meets her, she's never heard of God before. There is no sense in the Bible that Moses has shared with her about who the God of his ancestors is. Presumably, by the time Moses receives her as his wife and they journey together, something happens that Exodus does not record for us. We can imagine the kind of conversation Moses and Zipporah likely had on the journey. Just as God tells Moses that he's not returning for a family reunion, so Moses presumably reveals to Zipporah the purpose of the trip back to Egypt.

Zipporah apparently knows to be on the lookout for this God and understands the nature of the relationship between God and people. The relationship God wants with his people is like that of a father to a son and a spouse to a spouse. God is a protective, jealous spouse, as we will see when we discuss the commandments. God demands absolute loyalty and monogamy in the love relationship. Zipporah recognizes that Moses has failed to complete the task. He has agreed to follow God but has not lived up to the sign of the agreement—circumcision of his firstborn. If God and God's messenger are to be trusted, then Moses has to complete his responsibility to the covenant just like anyone else. Zipporah, a pagan Midianite, understands this agreement.

God renews an agreement with his people just like two spouses vow to stay together in a marriage. Just as a bridegroom pledges to his bride in covenant marriage, circumcision is the sign of a covenant between God and Moses. Circumcision of the firstborn son is the sign of the covenant, and Moses has failed in his responsibility. When God arrives, Zipporah is on the alert. She completes Moses' part of the bargain and saves Moses' life. She uses language suggestive of a marriage covenant: "You are a bridegroom of blood." She places their son's foreskin on Moses' "feet," a Hebrew euphemism for testicle.

If God is capable of igniting a bush, Zipporah assumes that Moses needs to beware. The people need to learn what God is capable of. Moses experiences firsthand what Abraham saw on Mt. Moriah with Isaac. This is a God who sends Abraham up on a mountain to sacrifice his son and then chooses to stop Abraham from killing Isaac. This is a God who sends a flood over the earth and promises never to destroy it again.

Reunion and Performance (4:27-30)

Just as God directs Moses' steps, so God orders Aaron to meet Moses in the wilderness. Their future home is also their place of reunion. Moses has survived an attack from God and is now reunited with his brother. God's messengers are now complete. Together they arrive to demonstrate what God can do. They journey to Egypt and "perform the signs in the sight of the people." Their demonstration is greeted with belief and worship. The people recognize that God hears their groans, and they're now prepared to follow these two to a new place of worship.

Lessons from an Uncontrollable God

Just when we think we have figured out God's motives, God surprises us with another aspect to God's character. This is no ordinary God. Yahweh speaks through a bush, sends messengers, seeks them out, and relents from God's plan. God dialogues, argues, and saves. God improvises with people like Moses, Zipporah, and Aaron who are vulnerable to everything that life can throw at them. If they can survive this kind of initiation, they'll be prepared for anything.

God loves to use deceitful people because God loves to use people. It's not just the deceitful ones like Moses that God uses. God loves everybody, and he takes us "just as I am." But God does not leave us there. God's love is so relentless that it comes after us in ways that defy expectation and even imagination. It's reckless and untamed. Moses not only encounters this dimension of God's character but somehow survives it with help from his wife.

God could do a lot of things, but God chooses not to do them. The only way we can make sense of a passage like this is through the blood of Christ. God's sovereignty and incarnation come together in Jesus. As Christians, we see God's work in the Old Testament through the eyes of the resurrection.

By doing so, we are able to interpret the vengeful, murderous sections of the Old Testament as only one chapter in the story of God's work of redemption. God's love is so relentless that, once we are compelled by it and constrained by it, God begins to change us. It is a love that transforms us in ways we can't begin to describe. We would like to know how God's love changes us, and we are good at pointing out how everybody else should change because of God's love. In some ways, God takes us just as we are—with all of our selfishness and jealousy and superiority. But God doesn't leave us there, and that's what Moses will experience. Because God's love is so overwhelming, Moses has a new perspective. He discovers the uncontrollable side of God's love. There are only two characters in the entire text who seem to have a hint of what God's uncontrollable love all about: the God that Moses is trying to serve in the best way he knows how and the wife that Moses marries.

1. What do you think the "bridegroom of blood" means?

_____

_____

_____

_____

_____

2. God's sovereignty and incarnation go together. How does the resurrection of Jesus change your perspective on this passage?

_____

_____

_____

_____

_____

3. Zipporah saves Moses' life. How does her demonstration of faithfulness inspire you?

_____

_____

_____

_____

_____

4. Try to write a "Zipporah monologue." Imagine her feelings, motives, and surprise on this journey of faith with Moses.

_____

_____

_____

_____

_____

Pharaoh:
Who Is Pharaoh?

Focal Text: Exodus 5:1–7:7

Above the entrance of the Dachau concentration camp, the Nazis placed a slogan, "*Arbeit macht frei*" or "Work makes (a person) free." I visited Dachau in 1992 on a study-abroad trip. The sinister nature of the sign reveals a deeper evil. Work paired with oppression leads to even worse bondage. Work with rest and worship, however, leads to friendship with Almighty God. In this chapter, Moses announces God's good news: a vision of God's divine plan that still liberates people today. Moses exposes Pharaoh's tactics and shows how the Israelite families reveal God's power over the king.

Work without Worship and Rest (5:1–6:1)

A PLACE TO WORSHIP (5:1-9)

Moses knows that Pharaoh's and Israel's needs are in opposition to each other. Pharaoh needs the cheap labor, and Israel needs to worship unhindered. Moses proposes a compromise to Pharaoh. Assuming Pharaoh will release the people, he asks for a three-day journey to a place in the wilderness where they can worship God. The slaves have power to oppose Pharaoh, but they do not recognize it. As we noticed in chapter 3, the Israelites allowed to worship; they just can't leave Egypt to do so. Additionally, Pharaoh and the Hebrews do not practice Sabbath, which is part of God's key command that forms the foundation of the Israelite structure of life.

THE COMPLICIT TASKMASTERS (5:10-21)

Pharaoh maintains his grip on power by enlisting the help of Hebrews to be middle management. By doing so, he divides the people and sets them against each other. The Hebrew bosses report Pharaoh's message to their people, and they are beholden to the king. They protect Pharaoh from directly interacting with his subjects. When the taskmasters try to serve as messengers to Pharaoh, he labels the people as lazy. He reveals his continual concern that giving the Hebrews a break from work will result in less power for himself. The taskmasters then turn on Moses and Aaron, accusing them of bringing this calamity upon the people. The Hebrew supervisors play both sides against one another in an attempt to protect themselves from the brutality of Pharaoh and from being forced to perform the nearly impossible task of making bricks without straw.

Appeal to God (5:22-23)

In Exodus 5:3, Moses and Aaron proposed a compromise to Pharaoh to allow the people to go into the wilderness for three days and return. But the compromise fails, and Pharaoh imposed even harsher work conditions on the people. Moses and Aaron appear to fail at diplomacy and negotiation. They're caught between a pharaoh who abuses people, taskmasters working both sides, and their own role as ambassadors to lead the people into the wilderness to rest. With no one else to turn to, Moses and Aaron turn to the Lord.

Moses and Aaron confront two realities: (1) God wants to deliver his people permanently from slavery. (2) Things often get worse before they get better. As Moses and Aaron get closer to the heart of Pharaoh's evil, the challenges become more complicated. They raise theological questions such as "Why have you mistreated this people?" (v. 22). Moses wants to know why God would send Moses to Pharaoh in the first place. The only way out of this "no-win" situation is for Moses and Aaron to lead the people out of Egypt.

A Freedom Vision (6:2-8)

Instead of bargaining with the oppressor, God presents a nine-fold plan of deliverance. This is both vision and call to Moses explaining how freedom works. God wants more than a three-day journey (5:3). He wants to deliver the Hebrews so that they can know who Yahweh is and likely so that the Egyptians can know who God is. As Isaiah suggests, God is appointing a people to be a "light to the nations" (Isa 42:6).

1. God will free the people from the burdens of the Egyptians. Just as Jesus said, "My yoke is easy and my burden is light" (Matt

11:30), God will now remove the weight of the Egyptians from the backs of the people.

2. God will deliver them from slavery. God will then take away their identity and occupation. Never more will they be indentured servants.

3. God will redeem them. "Redemption" is a marketplace word normally used to connote a purchase or exchange of goods. In this context, God claims God's people who had been enslaved by Egyptians. He redeems them from bondage and announces judgment on the Egyptians.

4. God will take the people. Even before they arrive at Mt. Sinai, God calls the people. They are "taken out." As the believers are taken out from among the Gentiles in Acts 15, so the Israelites are taken out from the Egyptians and set apart in Exodus.[1]

5. God will be their God. Just as God revealed to Abraham who God was, now God will continue that legacy with the Israelites.

6. The Israelites will know that God is their Lord. God is not only leading them but is also in relationship with them. They recognize God's works and follow.

7. God will bring them into the land. God's deliverance comes with a place. The Israelites will receive a space to occupy.

8. God will commit to them. God will renew a vow to them, much like a marriage relationship.

9. God will give to them. Ultimately, there is grace. They can't earn this status God has taken, brought, and now gives to them.

As Terence E. Fretheim says, this is the holistic gospel of Exodus. This is not just a liberation from something; it's a freedom *for* something. This is a commitment from an almighty God who is going to keep doing what God wants to do for God's people.[2]

Family Ties (6:9-27)

Despite Pharaoh's attempts to divide the Hebrews, God creates households who fear and serve him. This network of husbands, wives, and children becomes an unstoppable force as they depart Egypt. To accomplish the mission, God must continue to override their objections.

Moses' and Aaron's dress rehearsal before the Pharaoh did not go as planned (5:1-9). Despite their initial belief (4:30-31), the people remain unconvinced of God's power and Moses' abilities (6:9).

Moses himself lacks the self-confidence in his speaking to meet with Pharaoh (see 6:2-13, 30). Despite God's effort, the people and Moses still object. We are reminded that God's grace does not override human response. In the case of slaves, it takes a lot of work for people in bondage to unite. As Carol Meyers suggests, evil lurks within the divisions of the people as much as in the oppressors.[3] One of Pharaoh's ways of maintaining his power is to keep the people oppressed and sow discord among them against Moses.

God's plan runs deeper than human organizations; he uses fathers, mothers, and children. They do not require training in public speaking but rather faithfulness to the God of their ancestors. Notice a few of the names mentioned in the genealogy (6:14-26). We meet Jochebed, who is both Moses' and Aaron's mother and their great-aunt (6:20). We are introduced to Aaron's family: his wife Nahshon and sons Nadab, Abihu, Eleazar, and Ithamar. Ithamar will play a significant role later in the construction of the tabernacle. We meet Eleazar's wife, "one of the daughters of Putiel" (v. 25).

This genealogy links Moses' ancestors and traces redemption through his bloodline. Despite his personal failure, God uses his family. The family tree grows through the firstborn brother Aaron, previewing the priesthood that is to come. We learn Moses' father's name (Amram) and his mother's name (Jochebed) as well as the name of Aaron's wife, Elisheba. Even Moses' mother, Jochebed, was married to her nephew (a relationship later prohibited in the law). God works through flawed family systems and also names individuals in the process. In spite of human flaws, God somehow uses all of them.

Octogenarians Perform (6:28–7:7)

Moses still does not believe that the power of God can be seen through him. After he hears God's promises, and even after he learns about his family lineage, Moses remains skeptical. But God overrides Moses' disobedience with a word from his family.

The opening of chapter 7 reveals that an eighty-year-old knows more than the powerful Pharaoh. Moses knows what God can do. A senior adult will appear to be a god to Pharaoh. Moses has assumed that he will be a spokesman. In reality, he has been preparing to play a part in a dramatic performance of God's presence face to face with Pharaoh. The king of Egypt assumes that he is the all-powerful god. Now he is confronted by a God who can disguise himself as a stammering shepherd. What Moses is unable to realize is that when he appears in Pharaoh's court again, and with Aaron as a mouth-piece, the unknown Pharaoh will finally have met his match in a murdering shepherd who has returned to deliver his people.

Communicating the Calling

The nine-fold plan of deliverance illustrates a pattern in Exodus. Most things happen in sequences to help storytellers and older generations remember and retell the stories to others. There are five objections from Moses and five answers from God; seven ways God works behind the scenes; nine ways God will deliver the people; ten portents from creation; ten commands for survival.

As God's plan for deliverance continues to unfold, we learn important lessons in the ways God communicates God's message to the oppressors and the oppressed.

1. God's calling overrides human objections and responses. This is the final call of Moses. There will be no more negotiation or dialogue. God's call supersedes everything that Moses and the people can argue. When God has called a person to a task to fulfill God's mission, he uses such objections as preparation for a perfor-mance of his own work—not ours.

2. Performances before authorities are publicity for God. There is an old phrase in the marketing industry that holds true here: "All publicity is good publicity." Pharaoh's resistance to Moses' message plays right into the plan for the performance. God wants an audience in Pharaoh's palace in order for the message to be shared throughout the land. The stage of Pharaoh's court is the Egyptian equivalent of a public hearing on CNN. The performance is a marketing campaign. This is publicity for God to communicate a powerful message of presence to the people. If God is going to liberate the people from Egypt, God needs the word to leak through the halls of the palace that a new King is in charge. Moses and Aaron are advertising, and so are the people. As Pharaoh delivers them, and as the people respond, it gets the attention of the Egyptian people.

As we discussed in the previous session, Jesus prepared his disci-ples to appear before religious and political leaders (Luke 21:15).[4] Much like Moses in front of Pharaoh, their appearance resulted in publicity for the good news of the gospel and broad attention to their cause.

3. Supposed "enemies" will convert. God will not only get the attention of Pharaoh and the Israelites; a new revolution will also

begin in Egypt. The natives will know and trust this God as the Israelites are delivered. This witness is a form of evangelism that allows the name of God to be shared and spread throughout the Nile region. We should never dismiss an opportunity to demonstrate God's power when we're enduring suffering at the hands of taskmasters. Some will convert because of the faithfulness of God's people. Just as the disciples saw opportunities when they were arrested, so the book of First Peter also encourages Christians to live out their faith in a hostile environment. Exiled Christians would have opportunities that few others would have, and those would lead eventually to conversion (1 Pet 3:8-22).

4. Freedom not only comes with God's action; it comes with his promise and our responsibility. We follow, rest, and worship. Our lives are given over to God because God is the one who has saved us. We lose our identity in God and in God's mission if we fail to follow, rest, and worship. God renews his covenant with us by reminding us who God is and who we are. In case we do not remember, our acts of obedience reveal to others who God is.

5. God's nine actions to deliver the Israelites are still the way God works for us today. When God announces a vision of freedom, God also commits to these nine activities to deliver us. Despite what happens in our families, God is still working in us. Sometimes God is working in other members of our families in spite of us.

In bondage or deliverance, work doesn't liberate us. God's vision of freedom does, and we take on our assignments because of God's presence in our lives.

1. How have you seen God's freedom vision play out in your life? What responsibilities have you had to take on to participate in that vision?

_____

_____

_____

_____

_____

2. Moses learns that God was auditioning him to play the role of God to Pharaoh. Similarly, God uses us to show people who God is—not who we are. How does this perspective change your view of God's call?

_____

_____

_____

_____

_____

3. Who are the octogenarians in your life who have shown you God's power? How can eighty-somethings play a more active role in the life of your church?

_____

_____

_____

_____

_____

Notes

1. Terence Fretheim, *Exodus*, Interpretation (Louisville: John Knox, 1991), 93.

2. Fretheim, *Exodus*, 93.

3. Carol Meyers, *Exodus*, New Cambridge Bible Commentary (Cambridge: Cambridge University, 2005), 67.

4. William D. Shiell, "'I Will Give You a Mouth and Wisdom': Prudent Speech in Luke 21:15," *Review and Expositor* 112/4 (2015): 215.

Part 2

The Contest

(Exodus 7:8–15:20)

Fingers:
Who's in Charge?

Focal Text: Exodus 7:14–11:10

Americans love competitions. From reality shows to athletics, we are drawn into the stories of people's lives and the desire to be "world champion." We could say that competition is its own form of religious devotion.

The ancient world loved contests as well. Two warriors would fight in battle on behalf of an army and determine the victor. Could the same be said for a contest between God and Pharaoh? The book of Exodus tells the story of a great showdown between a god-like political figure who enslaved people and the one true God who, despite a prolonged silence, worked to free them. Moses uses this contest to convince Pharaoh to liberate the people and to motivate the Israelites to leave Egypt. The Israelites had already seen the power of Pharaoh, and they remained largely unconvinced that they should follow the shepherd Moses out into the desert.

The contest uses ten elements of creation to expose Pharaoh's tricks, demonstrate Egypt's death grip on the people, reveal that God is in charge of God's creation, and evacuate the people from the land. Through the contest, God reconstitutes God's people and cleanses creation of the effects of Pharaoh's regime. In the process, we receive a ten-lesson curriculum for helping future generations understand how God's power can change them.

The Fingers of God

We call the ten events "the plagues," but that is a misnomer. A plague suggests punishment or abuse. These events are portents of God's creative power. Most English versions of the Bible have led us to think that the "plagues" are God's way of punishing Pharaoh and the Egyptians. In reality, the word "plague" is only used three times in Exodus 7–11. When the Lord sends frogs to the Egyptians, the text uses the word "plague" as a verb: God *plagues* the people. Hail and the loss of firstborn are "plagues" because they end in the loss of life, but the other events are either signs or wonders. Signs point to the person, revealing the one who causes these calamities. Wonders are the evidence of divine intervention in human affairs, things that can only be explained the way the flummoxed magicians describe them—as the "finger of God" (8:19). They point to the God who is in charge of both Pharaoh and creation.

In order for the people to see God at work and to motivate Pharaoh to release them, God stages a living drama by using the wonders of creation and by using his actors Moses and Aaron. The signs and wonders reenact creation to restore order and reboot the system. They wipe the slate clean and exorcise the control that Pharaoh has on the minds and hearts of the people. They restore the way God wants the world to work.

These portents are for Exodus what the flood story is for Genesis—with one exception. The water of the flood cleanses the world and restarts creation with a new family to repopulate the world. In Exodus, God does not cleanse the world with water but uses the created order to reveal his power and release the people from the death grip of Pharaoh. Playing the part of God are Moses and Aaron. They strip away the illusion of Pharaoh's control in order to introduce people to the God of Abraham, Isaac, and Jacob.

We should study these events like they are divine object lessons for a people in bondage. Just as a science teacher uses experiments to teach a course, the signs, wonders, and plagues of Exodus are God's performances of his power. These activities disrupt the way people think life is ordered and reveal who's in charge. The Egyptian magicians can imitate the signs of water and frogs, but they're limited in their abilities. The "plagues" show people who the Israelites belong to. They're not Egyptians. They're the called people of Israel with a purpose to worship their God; God answers the big question of who God is with a demonstration of whose they are.

These events play out on the stage of creation: water, air, land, and living creatures. Two events feature water as the source of life: blood and frogs. Two show God's power on land: gnats and flies. Four dangers fall on living things: boils, pestilence, hail, and the death of firstborn children. Two happen in the air: locusts and darkness.

These events give both the Israelites and the Egyptians opportunities to turn to God. In the plague of locusts and the death of the firstborn, the Egyptians could save their livestock and their children by obeying God.

Collectively, each act builds on the other to release the people from bondage. Eight of them have a unique purpose in the drama either to inform the Israelites, the Egyptians, and Pharaoh or to train Israelites for greater purposes. Let's use this chart to explain the venue and purpose of each one.

Event	Venue	Purpose
Water to blood	Water	Who God is (7:17)
Frogs	Water	God is unique (8:10)
Gnats	Land	Finger of God—the natural world points to God (8:19)
Flies	Land	God's immanence—God is in the land (8:22)
Livestock	Created beings	God protects God's people (9:4)
Boils	Created beings	Unknown
Hail	Created beings	God is unique, more powerful than Pharaoh, and God wants to spread God's name and reputation to others, God will protect anyone who obeys God (9:16-19)
Locusts	Air	God wants children and grandchildren to learn these lessons (10:2)
Darkness	Air	Unknown
Death of firstborn	Created beings	God multiplies God's wonders (11:9)

Even though we could discuss each one in detail, let's focus on the locusts (10:1-7). Scientists at the United Nations tell us that in one day, locusts can consume the same amount of food as 2,500 humans. Locusts are so potent and deadly that they feed off the same thing humans eat. When it's the rainy season, locusts reproduce best when the crops are growing. As they leave an area, locusts lay their eggs so that the next group can come and lay waste to the same area.[1] In early 2020, swarms as long as 37 miles long and 25 miles wide swept across African countries including Ethiopia, Kenya, and Somalia.[2]

Why does God resort to locusts if this is the kind of havoc they wreak? This portent explains the rationale behind the wonders God is performing. God wants a curriculum to show future generations how foolish the Egyptians were to trust Pharaoh and to demonstrate to them who God is and what God is capable of (10:2). The "plagues" are a covenant-based curriculum for future generations in the wilderness, during the exile, and in congregations today.[3]

For generations, Pharaoh has used the Hebrew grandchildren as a workforce for his future projects. He sees immigrant children as the means to the Egyptians' ends rather than as God's images created for God's purposes. Now Pharaoh attempts to bargain with Moses and uses the children as pawns. He wants to let the men in the wilderness worship God (10:11) but leave the young people back home. Pharaoh learns that you can never bargain with children or grandchildren if you want to survive God. Children and grandchildren can't be used as leverage or hostages for any situation. God created them in God's image. They bear God's likeness for the future.

As David Brooks has written, Judaism and Christianity are "promise-centered" faiths. They are based on narratives that lead from Genesis through the unfolding revelation and glorious culmination. Believers' lives have significance because they are part of this glorious unfolding. Their faith is suffused with expectation and hope. If they believe life is a dead end, there is no purpose. Life has meaning and purpose because God has provided a future through their grandchildren. In Exodus, the hope of posterity plays an important role in evacuating the people so that they can have a future. The signs and wonders reveal a dead-end existence. To remain in Egypt is to turn their grandchildren into commodities for slave labor and to sentence them to die.[4]

God creates a multi-generational community that views grandchildren as just as significant in worship and decision-making as grandparents. Octogenarians lead the people to a desert worship center because they know this is the only way their posterity will survive. They have something important to teach them. Pharaoh, who has sacrificed their grandchildren for his building projects, will surrender his most important child to the Lord without redemption so that the people can learn that God owns everything.

Curriculum for Training Grandchildren

How does God intend for the Israelites to carry on for future generations? Each generation retells the story for those who were not there to experience it firsthand. As Walter Brueggemann wrote, "The number one job of grandparents is to help grandchildren remember."[5] The plagues name the pain the people are in and announce publicly that the struggle to leave is easier than the pain of staying in Egypt. By naming the "plagues," they learn to acknowledge the pain in their world so they can be ready to move forward into God's future.

God asserts dramatic power over creation to get Israel out of Egypt and to get Egypt out of Israel. Life is not good in Egypt, but it is predictable. The only thing worse than staying the same is human-initiated change. It's the reason families and churches remain stuck in dysfunctional patterns. The pain they know seems to be so much better than the uncertainty of change.

The drama of the plagues gives the Israelites the curriculum to expose the forces of death. Every generation will need a course designed to expose the darkness. By teaching the fingers of God, present and future generations will have a way of seeing the world as future events unfold. When natural and unnatural disasters happen, we learn how to use these events to point us to God and humble ourselves before God. Grandparents teach grandchildren how to surrender their power and trust in the God who created the water, air, land, and living creatures. We learn to trust that the God who sheltered obedient Egyptians and Israelites is the same God who invites us into an adventure with God to worship in the desert. By recognizing the pain we're in, we are able to discover that sometimes moving is the only way to save us.

In the dramatic contest between God and Pharaoh, we learn four powerful lessons that we can apply to our teaching today.

1. God's handiwork can be imitated. Magicians, scientists, inventors, and faith healers can often imitate things God can do. Life has plenty of benefits and blessings, and we can often get temporary spiritual relief from things and people other than God. Science can do many things that we ascribe to God's work. Medicine may temporarily heal our mortal bodies, but eventually we die.

Someone might say, "I don't need the church or God; I get my motivation and spirituality from other sources." Sometimes this is true, but all of these sources are temporary. Exodus reveals that without God's guidance, every blessing of life leads to death.

Exodus teaches how to view the blessings of our world today. Instead of trying to control the world, we trust in the God who is in charge of the world. Blessings such as health and safety are fingers pointing us to trust in God.

2. Emergency obedience without repentance is disobedience. In the plague of hail, Pharaoh obeys God and rescues his livestock (9:27). Like many people who pray for God to save them in a crisis, he is willing to obey for his own survival. True obedience, however, surrenders control of your life to God in humility, recognizing that God has the power to save and destroy. No matter what happens, God is in charge.

The same could apply to the Israelites or anyone else who has relocated their lives. Running from a terrible situation is only one part of the journey. Moving out of bondage does not automatically guarantee faith in God any more than a rescue prayer for deliverance.

For instance, we often advise people changing jobs not to run from a problem but focus their attention on what they are moving toward. If we only focus on what we're leaving behind, we can arrive at the new destination and fall back into bondage in other ways.

Exodus opens our eyes to see how a change in location can position us to allow God to work in our lives. The Israelites learn to be open to a God who wants to move with them on the journey. By moving into the wilderness, they have the opportunity to live into their identity as God's people.

3. God has power over the natural world, but the plagues are not God's normal operating system. The plagues illustrate what God can do, not what God normally does. Because they are a curriculum for faith, they show us the wonders of God's power. They teach us what God's capabilities are but not God's normal habits. Most of the time, God doesn't use the forces of nature as a way of teaching lessons to us. Instead, they are usually fingers to point us to him. God's normal mode of operation is rescue. He routinely suffers with people, evacuating people from their "Egypts" and leading them into a new place. Because God is a rescuer, God is willing to move heaven and earth to save those who trust in him.

The plagues help us see that when the world's operating systems are failing and God's people are being destroyed, God is willing to supersede the natural order and in some cases even use natural causes to assert his authority over the created world. God demonstrates God's control over creation, instead of wiping out the world as the pharaoh feared the gods would do. Pharaoh thought that, through his magicians, he could intimidate the Israelites by turning sticks into snakes, turning the sea red, and all the other tricks that magicians could do. But suddenly God brings new signs that no one can do. God demonstrates that the forces of nature testify to a God of life, not a God of destruction. All creation is not destroyed, and some people are saved.

4. *God's curriculum prepares us for a world that repeats itself.* Future Pharaohs will always attempt to enslave God's people, and the people will be tempted to remain in bondage. The plagues prepare the grandchildren of today to be the grandparents of tomorrow and teach the story to future generations. It should not surprise us when air, water, land, and living creatures are threatened by stubborn "pharaohs." They change their minds frequently and invoke God's name for their purposes. They're even willing to say "I have sinned" to save their own skin.

In response, we are to seek counsel from people who are Moses' and Aaron's age. As we learned in our last lesson, they are octogenarians (Exodus 7) exposing how Pharaoh has destroyed the created order. Senior adults have much to teach their children and grandchildren in the faith. They teach us to name reality for what it is. Despite the meager tools at our disposal, there is someone else working. Salvation is coming, and rescue is here. If you live and follow that promise in your life, then it will be fulfilled.

The "fingers of God" is a curriculum to interpret the events of 2020. We have been infected by biological and spiritual viruses. Covid-19, racism, police brutality, injustice, and sin have occurred simultaneously. Locusts plague Africa and Asia again. Using Scripture, we might be tempted to view these portents as "acts of God" or "tests of faith." There is another interpretation, however. We can view these events as part of the natural contest between good and evil. When they occur, they expose the evil forces that harm

God's people. In this season, we have learned that Black persons face intimidation and threats from police that most White persons never experience. We have also discovered that African American and Latino communities are disproportionately impacted by Covid-19.

The curriculum from Exodus invites children and grandchildren into deeper conversations about faith, justice, and redemption. We can use Exodus to point them to trust in the God who walks with us through suffering, delivers us from bondage, and invites us into the wilderness to worship and obey God.

1. How did God use the events we know as "plagues" to convince the people that they needed to leave Egypt?

_____
_____
_____
_____
_____

2. Describe a change in your life that you did not expect or want but that you needed to go through in order to survive. When you look back now, are you able to see God at work in the change?

_____
_____
_____
_____
_____

3. Name some of the pharaohs today that threaten our existence. How does the curriculum of the plagues give you confidence to replace your fears with confidence and faith?

_____
_____
_____
_____
_____

Notes

1. "'Rolling emergency' of locust swarms decimating Africa, Asia and Middle East," _The Guardian_, accessed June 8, 2020, theguardian.com/global-development/2020/jun/08/rolling-emergency-of-locust-swarms-decimating-africa-asia-and-middle-east

2. Rosie McCall, "Locust Swarms as Big as Cities are Causing a Crisis in Africa as Experts Warn They Could Get 400 Times Bigger," _Newsweek_, February 13, 2020.

3. Walter Brueggemann, "Antidote to Amnesia," in _Reclaiming the Imagination: The Exodus as Paradigmatic for Preaching_ (St. Louis: Chalice Press), 9.

4. David Brooks, "The Power of Posterity," *New York Times*, July 27, 2009, nytimes.com/2009/07/28/opinion/28brooks.html.

5. Brueggemann, "Antidote to Amnesia," 8.

Salvation: Questions God's Children Ask

7

Focal Text: Exodus 12:1–15:21

We mark history with the question, "Where were you when . . . ?" Remembrances of the tragedies and triumphs in life are recalled in conversations around the dinner table. Where were you when Kennedy was shot or when men walked on the moon? Where were you when the space shuttle *Challenger* exploded? What were you doing when you heard about planes flying into buildings in New York? Where were you when *Columbia* exploded? Where were you when Hurricane Katrina destroyed the lives of those on the coastline of Mississippi and Louisiana? Now, with Covid-19, What did you do during the pandemic? We will remember these days forever, and the memories will cause lasting pain for many of us. We add them to our story, and we walk through them over and over again.

Unlike moments we never forget, God's deliverance of the people through the sea is an ongoing movement. Exodus antici-pates that future generations will be retelling the story by asking not "Where were you when . . . ?" but "Why did this happen?" Without God's intervention, there is no Israel and there is no Christianity. But the incident at the sea is no mere flannelgraph story for us to recall from our Sunday school days. It is a picture of the way God's ongoing work of salvation opens pathways even today. It teaches us how to follow God while treating our supposed enemies the way God would want us to treat them. God takes the ordinary journeys of life and turns them into teachable moments for us to see God's glory and to participate in his cosmic redemption of creation. God places us in the next chapter of the story so we can continue to learn God's character and to follow God obediently.

Setting the Ceremony (12:1-28)

As God saves the people, God installs a ritual for traveling pilgrims. The meal commemorates the past and activates the events in the present. In other words, it brings the past into the present for the Israelites so future generations can be continually involved in the salvation message. Let's take a look at four features of the ceremony.

A NEW YEAR FESTIVAL (12:2)

Passover week starts the new year for the Israelites. Eventually, we will learn that the erection of the tabernacle accompanies the festival (Exod 38–40). Food, liturgy, and God's presence come together to start the year.

THE WHOLE CONGREGATION (12:3-11)

The entire congregation is involved in the preparation, celebration, and observation. For a week the people prepare a lamb without blemish, smear the doorposts with its blood, and eat the lamb as a meal. Children are involved in the ceremony (v. 26) and play a role in asking what the observance means. The community activities function as public invitations to Egyptians. They observe the signs on the doorposts and have the opportunity to participate in their own deliverance.

REMEMBRANCE AS OBEDIENCE (12:14)

Remembrance is active participation in God's salvation. By remembering, they are choosing to obey the God that brought them out of Egypt. They reenact the last night in Egypt and prepare their lives for the next phase of the journey ahead. Remembrance is not nostalgia for the past; it activates the past to call us to represent God's work in the present. Remembering calls upon God to deliver people from slavery and to continue the ongoing work of redemption.

LITURGY BEFORE SALVATION (12:25)

The Passover festival is a prescribed liturgy (public work) designed to be practiced before release. Worship precedes deliverance. The meal gives the people a framework for understanding liberation and provides a script for them to explain to their children and grandchildren why they survived (see 12:27). The meal legitimizes their salvation and their identity to posterity.

The meal is also a "to-go" meal for fearful pilgrims preparing to move.[1] God provides a framework in the midst of fear so that when it's time to evacuate, they are prepared to go where God sends them.

Skipped Over (12:29–13:22)

Moses has prepared the people to trust God with their lives. They make a meal to take with them in case Pharaoh releases them to the wilderness. With the people prepared for the final plague, God completes the process of evacuation. God kills the firstborn of every Egyptian household, even down to their livestock (12:29). The Hebrew word for Passover literally means "skipped over." The only ones spared are those who smear the lamb's blood on the doorpost of their houses. This plague is a mystery. We certainly don't understand why executing children and livestock is necessary. We do know that the one thing the Israelites take from this experience is a celebration that they have survived. Suddenly death doesn't reign over everyone.

Salvation in Exodus involves full participation in the divine deliverance and adventure that God has planned. Many people explain salvation as a private decision made between the individual and God. By contrast, salvation in Exodus is a divine activity. It requires community action in order to be accomplished. By preparing the meal, smearing the doorposts, and leaving when they are told, the people participate in God's plan for relocation and worship.

They follow God's lead down an unexpected path that can't be predetermined (13:17). God leads them down a circuitous road through the wilderness to the banks of the Red Sea, a marshy, reedy section of land (the Hebrew phrase is "Reed Sea"). The landmark serves as the political, spiritual, and geographical barrier between a life under Pharaoh's control and a new world with God in charge. Their surrender to a pillar of fire by night and a pillar of cloud by day previews what their lives and ours often become. Life is full of barriers to cross—some of which are caused by God and others happen because of our own decisions. The Israelites choose to follow God no matter who chose to cross the sea from this place.

There is a difference, however, between survival and salvation. Survival is a rescue operation that allows a person to go back to the way life used to be with no strings attached. Often, survival comes out of a desperate plea for help. Salvation, as Jews understood it and as Christians eventually perceived from the history of Israel, begins in rescue and ends with a complete change of lifestyle. Salvation causes us to recognize that we've been spared the disasters that befell others and to move with God through a wide space into a new way of living under God's guidance. The next act will be true deliverance.

Stand Still (14:1-14)

As they approach the banks of the sea, God tells Moses where to camp and causes Pharaoh to pursue the people. God stages a cosmic conquest to give the people a story to tell future generations about God's military power over enemies. The unarmed Israelites panic, assuming that they are trapped. Ironically, Pharaoh, Moses, and Aaron are now the only ones in the story who believe God is capable of destroying them. Pharaoh has seen God's power and experienced it. Now he rushes headlong into battle to wipe out the people that brought death to his palace. He fears death so much—and believes God can cause it—that he wants wipe out the people so they will never bring death back to him again. He attempts to use violence to end the threat.

Once again we're faced with the question of purpose: why is it necessary to engage in this kind of battle? There is a fine line between a dead end and a red sea. From their perspective, the Israelites are at a dead end and Pharaoh has trapped them. But from our perspective, God is everywhere. God is in charge of the direction the Israelites travel and also in charge of the hardness of Pharaoh's heart. God is still working to convert the pharaoh; he wants "to gain glory for myself over Pharaoh." God wants Pharaoh to surrender his power and thereby save the Egyptians and the Israelites. Pharaoh responds with the frenzied attempt to hang on to the power he never had. No one—not even the Israelites—believes the Lord yet. Moses responds with a paradoxical set of instructions: stand still and watch (14:14). Over the course of Exodus, we learn that God equips the Israelites to do several things in the face of imminent disaster. Instead of being afraid or resentful, God teaches them ten important movements:

1. *Prepare a meal.* The Israelites learn to trust God through food. God teaches them to prepare a meal for departure from Egypt, provides manna and quail (16:12), fellowships with Moses and Aaron on the mountain (24:11), and designs a table for bread in the tabernacle (25:23-30).
2. *Stand still and watch.* God fights for the Israelites against Pharaoh's armies in Exodus 14 and against the Amalekites in Exodus 17:8-13. God sends an angel warrior ahead of them in Exodus 23:20-33.

In each case, the Israelites learn to watch and obey. They do not fight with weapons of war but with allegiance to God.

3. *Remember God's work, and remind God of his faithfulness to you.* In addition to the work that happens at Passover, God remembers the Israelites in 2:23-25. The Israelites view Sabbath as a remembrance day (20:9-11).

4. *Go forward.* These pilgrims are on the move, and so is God.

5. *Worship.* God redeems the Israelites to worship God freely in the wilderness.

6. *Construct a building.* A critical activity on the journey is designing and constructing the space where they will worship God. The design process is an act of faith and obedience.

7. *Smear your doorposts.* By spreading blood, they are showing their neighbors publicly their true identity as God's children.

8. Sacrifice your first fruits and give your best sacrifice. The Israelites show their trust in God by giving generously of their time, talent, and treasure (34:8; 35:22).

9. *Rest.* Sabbath is a public way to demonstrate their trust in God for daily provision.

10. *Teach your grandchildren.* As we learn in Exodus, these lessons are to be used to train future generations.

This is a "stand still" moment for the Israelites. The Lord calls the Israelites to stand still and to watch God work (see Ps 46:10). As they stand, they notice God's incredible movement. Standing still gives them time to reflect, reconnect, and see God's work.

Salvation through the Sea (14:15-30)

Suddenly the mood shifts to a second movement—walking forward. God even asks, "Why are you asking me to do anything? Walk forward." When the Israelites are backed up to the Red Sea, Moses stretches out his hand. Instead of conquering the chaos, God divides the chaos into two parts. First, the people are left to do one thing— to walk forward. Second, the Egyptians, still consumed by their desire to fight a battle against an enemy that never existed, only consume themselves. They choose to walk forward right into the middle of the chaos. What was dry land is now mud. What was a place of salvation is now a place of death.

When the Israelites finally reach the other side and Moses stretches out his hand again for the final time, it is only then that they fear the Lord. As Brevard Childs noted, the people never believed until the moment of deliverance.[2]

Salvation identifies the evil in the world, accounts for it, and says, "God is going to move the people forward through these difficult situations." Instead of going around the chaotic waters of the sea, God divides them much like God divided the waters in Genesis 1. He separates them into two parts to create a space for people to walk through their situation. Just as in life the only way through a situation is often to go through it, God leads the Israelites through their fear. When they obey and follow, God delivers them and wipes out Pharaoh.

Both the Israelites and the Egyptians see the power of God, but only one group understands the act as God's act of creation. The Egyptians wanted to use God's power to wipe out the Israelites— just as they had used Pharaoh's power to enslave them. The Israelites, on the other hand, are willing to walk without knowing what will happen next.

Sing and Dance (15:1-21)

Safely on the other side, the Israelites sing and dance a psalm of salvation (15:2). The first part is led by Moses, and the prophetess Miriam sings in verses 20-21. Moses sings, "The LORD is my strength and my might, and he has become my *salvation*." At its root, the Hebrew word "salvation," or "Yeshua," means "to make wide" or "to make spacious." In Hebrew, the word is used as a verb (354 times) much more often than as a noun (146 times).[3] For the Hebrews, there is no difference between a mental decision to follow and the material notion of deliverance through a wide geographical point. It's all one spiritual-material transformation. Salvation takes the tight space that the Israelites are in and makes it wider. God brings something freeing into a tight human situation. Salvation creates the space for God to work.

In verse 3, the song praises God as a "warrior." Let's discuss what that term means in this context. God is not a warrior in the sense of a terrorizing bully. God values merciful acts of salvation. Instead of engaging in a battle to punish the world, God uses the forces of nature to save the world from the forces of darkness. God moves the people to a new place.

God redefines what it means to fight against an enemy army. The Israelites are unarmed pilgrims who either stand still or walk forward. That makes God a warrior of mercy, not of hate or vengeance. God is not about settling scores; God sends mercy and acts redemptively for the world. As Moses and the people sing in verse 13, "In your steadfast love (*hesed* in Hebrew), you led the people who you redeemed; you guided them by your strength to your holy abode."

Moses previews the character of God that will be more fully expressed in Exodus 33:19: "I will have compassion on whom I will have compassion. I will have mercy on whom I have mercy." God's battle is a war of mercy. Out of his burning mercy, God causes the water currents to stir and makes space.

Survival Lessons

The scene of the people passing through the sea points us to several lessons for a life of trust and faith in God today.

1. Salvation is moment and movement. Salvation doesn't begin with contrition. It begins with a meal in the midst of fearful, awe-inspiring times. When creation is in upheaval, we pass the lamb chops and rehearse the script. Salvation retells and retouches the story and the objects of our deliverance.

Salvation is more than a momentary survival. Praying for God's rescue is no different from making a desperate appeal for help after we've been caught. We might get out of a jam, but rarely do we change our lives. Salvation means that God moves toward us in the real and present circumstances of our lives—most of which are just ordinary moments like making bread and passing the meat to one another. Remember that salvation begins with the birthing room of ordinary women like Shiphrah and Puah. They were just doing their jobs. We don't have to relocate from where we live to understand that God is always moving and transforming us. God says, "I am present and accounted for. Now will you remain faithful to follow my presence?"

2. Faith walks people through the troubled waters. Faith is not what we use to escape trouble. Faith is the way we walk through the trouble in life because we believe that God is about the movement of salvation. Faith is more than just a hand receiving or taking what God gives us in deliverance. God gets into the world and our circumstances. Faith is also about saying, "Yes, God, I receive what the world gives, and I grab on to you as we go through the chaos."

There are two hands of faith. One cries out to God for rescue: "God, get me out of this mess." And God grabs us and delivers us.

The other hand clasps onto God in order to follow and serve God. When people fear the Lord, they're willing to cling to the God who rescues them. This willingness to hang on to the Lord is inspired by the sense that we are actively participating in the drama. There is no sense in Exodus of the cliché, "Let go and let God." Instead it is, "I'm grabbing on to the God who has been dragging me along this entire time."

Rather than removing us from the trouble we are in, God brings something into the human situation that is not already there. I AM THAT I AM enters and is present with us in the conditions; God doesn't abolish the conditions. The circumstances stay the same. The ordinary (bread, salt, work, moving) partners with the miraculous (Red Sea). All of them can be fingers of God.

3. God uses destruction to show mercy. The purpose of the Red Sea was not to defeat Pharaoh—it was to convert him. God wants glory because God is in charge and no one else can stand before God. God wants to define the world on God's terms again. God preserves that world as best he can. He even tries to preserve Egyptians who would trust and believe in what God is doing. The magicians recognize God's power even if they do not fully place their faith in God. In the same way, our salvation cannot be defined in terms of who we are against or who God is saving us from. If anything, we are saved from someone or something that enslaved us in order for the enslaver to have the opportunity to see and know God's power in us. The act of deliverance is a witness of God's power evangelistically.

4. The greatest threat is not our human enemies. If God is a warrior of mercy, then that means our enemies are never those we think we are fighting. For the Israelites, the enemy was never the Egyptians or their slave taskmasters. The enemy is always the evil that masks itself throughout creation and threatens our existence. We are in the midst of a cosmic upheaval. This enemy would like for us to treat humans as the ones we should destroy. Instead, the deliverance at the sea reveals that only God can rid the world of darkness and death. Egyptians were trying to destroy creation. When others would raise a sword, though, God simply blows his breath at this kind of evil. God's merciful weapon of forgiveness arms us with the greatest force that defeats the enemy even today.

5. Jesus is a picture of what God does through Passover and the Red Sea. In a sense, Jesus absorbs the Passover into himself. He participates in the Passover meal just as he has done his entire life. As he reenacts the Passover with his disciples, he instigates a way for believers to activate the Last Supper for posterity. The meal unites the believers with ancient Israel. Christians are also being skipped over. For the future, the meal becomes an act of remembering that Jesus is the sacrificial host. "This do in remembrance of me" means that God delivered the people from Egypt and is still delivering us. The Last Supper for Jesus becomes a New Year Festival for the believer (Luke 22: 13-20; Matt 26:19-30).

In the face of disaster or trouble, God calls the church today to be proactive and obedient rather than reactive and fearful. Just as the Israelites had a ten-step disaster plan, so the church should have one too.

1. *Hospitality and fellowship:* Prepare meals for people who have been through disasters. Run errands, and care for those who cannot help themselves.
2. *Wait:* Stand still and watch God's deliverance. We observe those first responders and essential workers. They are God's agents of healing and rescue. We pay attention to the ways God is working in seen and unseen ways.
3. *Pray:* As we remember God's work, we actively remind God of his faithful to work to us and remind each other of God's faithful work in our past.
4. *Step out in faith:* Recovery from a disaster requires bold innova-tion. We move forward in new directions trusting that God will accompany us through the decision-making process.
5. *Worship.* We maintain a rhythm of worship in the midst of crisis. Either gathered with a local church or scattered in homes, we remain faithful in worship.
6. *Design and build:* Just as we move forward in faith, we imagine the new work that will need to be done after disaster. We listen carefully to those in pain and design facilities and programs to be instruments of God's presence.
7. *Publicly witness to your neighbors:* The Israelites smeared their doorposts; our public witness happens in our neighborhood and on social media. We show and identify publicly with God.
8. *Give generously:* Disaster and deliverance are times to give gener-ously to those who have needs. Congregations take care of one another and their communities in creative, tangible ways.
9. *Keep Sabbath:* Even in a crisis, we need to take Sabbath in order to be better prepared to respond to issues.

10. Train others: We use the times of disaster and deliverance to teach future generations about God's power.

Here's one example in my life when I learned a bit about the two hands of salvation. When my older son, Parker, was a fifth grader, we explored the Sweetwater caverns called "The Lost Sea." Led by an expert guide and joined by a group of ten royal ambassadors (RAs) from the church, we climbed over the red clay mud through tight crevices. At one point, our guide led us through a cleft in the rock. He warned us in advance not to look down. We would simply need to squeeze through a tight space between two large boulders. When we reached the other side, the guide would be there to take our hand; we would step on a small rock and keep moving. This is not exactly the way it happened. I went first. Parker was holding my right hand, and I was maneuvering through a tight space. When I got halfway across, I realized I was about to either be stuck or fall through to the cavern below us. The guide shouted, "Give me your hand!" I grabbed his hand and dragged Parker through the boulders without even giving him a chance to stop. I stepped on a small rock and kept moving.

To me, this is like the two hands of salvation. I needed to walk forward, and the guide needed to pull me through. At the same time, I was pulling Parker along to safety. God does the same for us. God grabs onto us, we grab onto God, and we pull others along with us. We don't go around the boulders; we go between them and trust that God knows where God's leading us.

1. How does God continue to save people after they have decided to follow God? What responsibilities do we have to participate in that salvation movement?

_____

_____

_____

_____

_____

2. One of the key parts of the Israelite liturgy is eating. What are some of your favorite rituals around meals? How do these meals prepare you for God's work?

_____

_____

_____

_____

_____

3. Review the ten practices that churches can use today in the face of difficulties and disaster. Which ones does your church actively participate in today? Have you neglected any that need to be prioritized?

_____

_____

_____

_____

_____

Notes

1. John Durham, Exodus (WBC 3; Waco: Word Books, 1987), 156.

2. Brevard S. Childs, The Book of Exodus: A Critical, Theological Commentary (Louisville: Westminster John Knox Press, 2004), 238.

3. Eugene Peterson, Christ Plays in Ten Thousand Places: A Conversation in Spiritual Theology (Grand Rapids: Eerdmans, 2008), 172.

Salvation: Questions God's Children Ask

Part 3

The Journey
(Exodus 15:22–24:18)

Provision and Rest: How Can They Help Us?

Focal Text: Exodus 15:22–16:36

A rescue saves lives but also reveals character flaws. No sooner have the Israelites cleaned up from the victory party than they start complaining about the conditions in the desert. A food crisis often leads to a faith crisis. Once the Israelites are delivered, they realize that the Passover meal is insufficient to sustain them to the promised land. For Exodus, the promised land is not the destination—God's presence in the desert is. The people had one mission: to leave Egypt to worship God. Beginning with the end of chapter 15, the mood and tone shift from celebration to reality. Now God will test the people (and vice versa!), to prepare them for a new identity and equip them for the rough road to come.

The Israelites prefer a return to "normal," but they discover that the rules and situations of the wilderness are not anything like they imagined. In the wilderness, God uses the natural conditions of life to unleash God's abundant provision for the people. God also tests God's congregants to see if they will trust that God's daily provisions are enough. So, on a "normal" day in the wilderness, God opens their eyes to see daily provision through the natural world. They have seen God work supernaturally; now God works with creation and time to shape them into God's people.

People Grumble about Salvation (15:22–16:3)

Let's review how the Israelites arrived. The plan seemed simple: load up your few belongings to prevent the Egyptians from looting what you leave behind. The relocation process took about a month. God brought deliverance and demonstrated to them that salvation is much more than a moment. It's a movement of lives to a new destination.

After little more than a month of freedom, the Israelites complain. Even in the best of times, they mumble against leaders and groan in their deliverance. The words sound familiar. The language is dramatic, but it's also realistic. They need water, but they also groan about their wants. Their memories quickly become more desirable than their dreams or their realities. They have nostalgia for a time that never existed. They remember the few good times in the "good old days" of slavery when they sat around large pots of meat and ate all they wanted. Whether or not this was true, it was certainly their perception (16:3). And they blamed the only two guys who could help them—Moses and Aaron.

According to Exodus, more than half a million people and several cattle and livestock left Egypt to worship center in the wilderness. But a new destination does not transform minds. Memories can function in two ways. People can reminisce about a life they never had or remember the purpose of the journey they are taking. God spoke of a new home and destination, but the primary purpose was to shape them as people. Once they cross the Red Sea into the plains of Sinai and prepare to trek into the land, the journey suddenly comes to a halt. The people are worn out and weary, and they worry about what they will eat. Moses, who is not gifted as an administrator, is at his wits' end.

God Answers Prayer Naturally (16:4-21)

In response to the people's grumbling, God provides for and tests his "congregation" (16:9) (*ekklesia* in Greek). He "rains bread" on them the same way he rained locusts on the Egyptians. I love this image: God pummels them with provision. When the rain dries, a flaky, frost-like resin is left behind and drops from the thorns of the tamarisk tree. The people don't know what to call it so they ask, "What is it?" or in Hebrew, "Manna?" The second natural occurrence is birds. God sends a flock of quail to cover the camp (16:12).

God's provision comes with a test. God sends more than they could ever need for the day. He wants to see if they can trust that God will provide what they need daily, without becoming hoarders. No one would call the Israelites greedy, but greed's cousin is "security." The Israelites gather more food than needed because they are afraid that they will starve to death. When threatened, the Israelites hoard. Fearful that the substance will never return, they protect their people at the expense of others. Instead of trusting in God, they place their families above God. Everyone who gathers exactly what they need rather than what they want has plenty. But those who gather too much discover that there's no such thing as preservatives or refrigeration in the wilderness (16:21).

Time as an Antidote for Distrust (16:22-36)

To build trust and prevent further disobedience, God institutes a practice still in existence today. God knows that Israel needs margins and boundaries to give them protection against fear and greed. Instead of doing more supernatural work—like parting the Red Sea—God creates space in the rhythm of their week. God carves out the Sabbath on the seventh day. The people haven't even received the law yet, and God is already training them to rest. As Abraham Heschel wrote, the Sabbath was a "palace in time."

The people go out on the seventh day to discover no manna (16:27). Frustrated again with their disobedience, Moses chastises them and institutes the Sabbath rest (16:29). The Israelites signify Sabbath with a symbol:

> Moses said, "This is what the LORD has commanded: 'Take an omer of manna and keep it for the generations to come, so they can see the bread I gave you to eat in the wilderness when I brought you out of Egypt.'" (16:32)

Moses and Aaron find a jar for an omer, which is about a half-gallon. They place manna inside the jar. As they wander, the omer reminds them, "God took care of us in the moment of greatest need."

Sabbath as a Time to Trust

Exodus is a practical retelling of reality. The first time the Sabbath is practiced is not on a holy mountain or on a retreat. Sabbath is first observed when people are worried that the food God just provided is going to run out. Miracles are usually reserved for the unexplainable. As Fretheim suggests, they fit under the category "acts of God" because there is no other way to explain their occurrence.[1] Sabbath is no miracle. It's a gift that requires our work. God has already provided the time; we have to follow the routine. We learn several things about people's behavior regarding the Sabbath and rest that deserve further reflection.

1. Sabbath requires a lot of preparation. As Marva Dawn writes, the Israelites can't just slam on the brakes and expect to rest comfortably. Instead, they must spend all week working to get ready to cease. They prepare to stop so that the rest can be renewing. As the Israelites are brought into this wilderness, they suddenly realize that God is also a normal, everyday kind of God; God wants to eat with them in the wilderness. God says, "Let's just eat something here—naturally, normally."[2]

2. Sabbath gives us control over our time. The Israelites were able to stop their work in order to show that someone else was in charge. They didn't manage time; they observed it. They saw that there was an order and wonder to creation. One day each week, the world needed a break from them, and they needed to rest from creating. God said to them, "You must do some work to gather what you need but not hoard it. Know that I'll take care of you. I've already made you a success. The work will be there when you get back. I'll be there for you."

God says there are some things we can't hoard. There are some things we can't stockpile. Love: we can't store that up for a rainy day; it must be used every day. Friendship: we can't decide to be a friend today and not tomorrow; we can't say we'll start being friendly in a few years. Forgiveness: we can't say, "I'll start being gracious to others after several years of being forgiven." Time: we can't ever get that back; we'll always be using it.

3. Sabbath breaks our accustomed patterns. Instead of working harder, the Sabbath allowed the people to work smarter and more sustainably. They could take control of their time and not their jobs. When we feel helpless as employees, Sabbath is an act of resistance to human authorities as well as a sign that we serve a Higher Power. Sabbath replaces the constant churning of our lives to remind us how God leads us.

4. Sabbath reminds us who we are and where our identity comes from. The Israelites were not measured by all the things they did the other six days of the week. They were not primarily identified by their occupations as farmers, bricklayers, and straw makers. Like them, we find our identity as God's "congregation."

5. The food crisis for the Israelites is a picture of the crises we face. Like the Israelites, we should not be surprised that in the midst of deliverance, we also encounter challenges. We might face natural disasters, gas shortages, stock fluctuations, and health issues. Some are short-term problems; others we never quite get over. No matter the crisis, God provides two things for us—an abundance of what we need (daily bread and meat) and time (Sabbath).

6. People blame their deliverers. Moses, Aaron, Miriam, and eventually Bezalel and Joshua lead the people out of their worst condition. They also face blame and grumbling from their own people. They sabotage their leaders in 16:3, accusing Moses and Aaron of attempting to kill them in the wilderness. This kind of sabotage is the sign that Moses and Aaron are successful deliverers.

7. Leaders operate out of a sense of vulnerability. Deliverance reveals how dependent we are on God and how little we know about the direction we're headed. While most leadership and management books focus on strategic plans, Christian leaders recognize that vision is only discovered through a healthy sense of dependence on God and a desire to admit that they don't know what to do with the people they are leading. Moses and Aaron discover that there are no pre-programmed plans. They have to adapt along the way to the problems that occur. As Lewis and Clark discovered on their journey to map out the Louisiana Purchase, at some point we have to ditch the canoes and climb mountains. Moses and Aaron will change tactics many times in order to reach the point of worshiping God in the wilderness.

8. When we arrive, the destination is often not what we imagined. God tells Moses and Aaron to lead people out to the desert to worship God. There is no other place that God imagines at this point for the people. Later, we will learn about their conquest of Canaan (Josh 1:10-18). But leaders are reminded that they lead people to the next point along the way. If God opens doors to a new place, then so be it. Our role is to be faithful to the task that is set before us and to follow God's leadership through struggles, whether with the people or with the provisions.

9. Crises reveal the places and things in which we have placed false expectations. Just as the Israelites wanted the comfort of having extra bread, some people tend to hoard supplies and focus on security at the expense of others. This can happen during natural disasters like hurricanes, or in the case of Covid-19, when toilet paper and hand sanitizer became scarce. Such events reveal the worst and the best in humanity. For example, some people may hoard supplies when others clearly need those supplies as well. Crises can bring out the best in people: volunteers arrive, people donate supplies, many people want to help. Nurses come out of retirement to treat patients in hospitals. Even on a normal day in the wilderness, we can trust that God's going to be there and we're going to see God.

10. God's provisions come with a test. The church in North America faces a test similar to the one the congregation of Israel faced. We've been entrusted with much more than we could ask or imagine, and we've hoarded our wealth, assuming we'll need it for a rainy day. God wants us to trust God as the God of daily abundance and provision and to give so that others may live.

11. Sabbath is a means to set boundaries. God instituted Sabbath after deliverance when the Israelites were beginning to live into their newfound freedom. The first sign of their identity as people after crossing the sea was not be their name or their land; it was their time. God first gave them a meal and then gave them a schedule.

When we get a new job and relocate, the tendency is to work overly hard to make a good first impression. By observing Sabbath, we're able to stop and recognize that life and work and new freedom is a process.

We are workers. We work hard. We work longer hours. Many of us are familiar with the recent terms "side hustle" and "gig economy" because we're living them. In this passage from Exodus, we learn that the best way to testify to God's work in our lives and our trust in God is to cease from our labors. God says, "If you truly want to acknowledge my daily presence in your life, if you want to be able to sleep at night, you'll do the one thing that you can do, the one thing that you have control over: you will surrender control, not of your work but your time."

God gave Sabbath before God prescribed worship. That means that even when we can't worship on the Lord's Day, we can still observe Sabbath. However, worship should not be neglected. Both Sabbath and worship together renew our journey with God. Ceasing, reflecting, and allowing God to renew creation is a part of our worship but can never replace it. This should be a good reminder to those who went to church on Sunday and then went back to the office or to those who are at a child's ball game on Sunday but not worshiping. Sabbath and worship are two sides of a coin that need to be vigilantly monitored and tended.

The gift of Sabbath is designed to be a public ceremony of trust in God, that I can step away from the thing that both causes me stress and is my greatest source of provision. For some of us, that is our work, depending on our jobs. If your work is your family, they might be both your areas of stress and provision. The Lord says to take a break from the thing that increases anxiety. "Fill that time with simple things," God says. Like throwing a rock in the stream; taking a long walk in the woods; going to a hospital and visiting someone; sitting with a nursing home resident who doesn't know your name; spending time with a child. All of these things are God's incredible gifts of what we call Sabbath.

It isn't that we simply stop what we are doing. As Jesus reminded us, we should fill our break with good things so that we can remind ourselves how God leads us. Unless we are able to cease from the normal activity of everyday life, we will never be able to look back and see God's daily provision of leading us by God's hand.

As a result of the Covid-19 pandemic, we are truly living in a new normal. We would like to know when we can go back to life the way it was before the pandemic, but we likely never will be the same again. We also do not know when the pandemic will subside. So in the midst of the disaster, we need to stop. We reflect over the last several months and we say, "This is where the Lord was. This is where God is working in the daily activities of life."

12. Deliverance often requires waiting in stages. The tendency for many people after a sudden change or loss is to just keep moving. But the Israelites show us that moving forward can cause us to bypass the important work God wants to do while we wait. In order to get to the promised land, we must go through the wilderness. God leads us into the wilderness and wants to use this landscape as an opportunity to prepare us for God's presence.

"Can't we get on with this journey?" we might ask. "Can't we just keep going? Why not just move this train along and keep these people rolling? Why stop now? It's a lot of trouble to carry an extra jar with us. It's a lot of mess to stop and set everything down; it's just easier to keep moving."

The symbolic jar, the omer of manna, that the Israelites carried was made real to me when I pastored at First Baptist in McGregor, Texas. This was a small church. We did not have annual budget and money concerns. We were concerned with the offering weekly and monthly. One of the ways God provided was through the life of Lester Little. Lester was a member of my church, but he attended every church. Each week, you'd see Lester riding around town on his bicycle. He was a Sabbath sort of guy because he didn't like to drive; he just liked to give. Lester would pick up pennies and loose change, items that most people would drop in the streets in their rush to get onto the next thing, and whenever a church would get ready for a building program, he would donate a jar of his pennies to that church. Most of the time, Lester would slip in the back or attend an evening service. Most of the time, he toured around and checked all the preachers out. And even when one of the preachers in McGregor left and moved on to a big church in Richardson, Texas, the first person there to make a donation to the building campaign was Lester Little with his huge jar of pennies. When I was serving at the little church, we received word one morning that Lester had been struck and killed by a car while picking up his pennies. If anything, it was Lester's way to go. But today, if you go to First Baptist Richardson, they still have that jar of pennies in the church library to remind them that, when they needed it the most, God provided for them through a little man on a bicycle, a man who truly brought God's Sabbath provision to life.

1. What do you do to prepare to rest on the Lord's Day?

_____

_____

_____

_____

_____

2. What kind of break/ceasing/resting can happen each day?

_____

_____

_____

_____

_____

3. Reflect on the provision jar that Moses asked the Israelites to keep. If you were to place something in a mason jar at home to display as a reminder of God's provision for you, what would that be?

_____

_____

_____

_____

_____

4. Many people in nursing homes and assisted living centers have a Sabbath every day. No longer bound by a work schedule, they wait patiently for others to come and renew them. How can you use the Sabbath to renew others?

_____

_____

_____

_____

_____

Notes

1. Terence Fretheim, *Exodus*, Interpretation (Louisville: John Knox, 1991), 184.

2. Marva Dawn, *Keeping the Sabbath Wholly: Ceasing, Resting, Embracing, Feasting* (Grand Rapids: Eerdmans, 1989), 23.

Sessions with Exodus

Tests of Leaders:
Is the Lord among Us?

S e s s i o n

Focal Text: Exodus 17:1–18:27

Every relationship gets stretched with time. A couple married for fifty years relates to each other differently on their golden anniversary than on their silver one. In our text, God and Israel are early in their renewed commitment to each other. God had called the people but had not yet constituted them as a nation. Wilderness strengthens their commitment to the mission. Wilderness is their mutual boot camp into the life of following God. In this place, the Israelites test two leaders: the God who rescues them and the man God appoints to lead them. Just as God has tested them and will continue to test them through their growth in God, the Israelites put God to the test with a simple question—"Is the LORD among us or not?" God responds by changing Moses' leadership style with some help from family. We learn to view the wilderness as necessary for a life of faith.

Tests in the Wide Space (17:1-16)

Historians tell us that the Israelites were likely not the only ones migrating through the Middle East at this time. During the Exodus era, several people groups relocated because of changing climate and new weapons technology that fortified defenses for formerly helpless tribes. It makes sense then that God would be involved in this migration and send a tribe of supposedly helpless people without a standing army to demonstrate God's power. Ironically, God sends people with meager weapons—just swords—and no military tactics to demonstrate God's power. God leads them into literally a wide place in the road so they can confront God and so God can show them that God is battle tested.

Water in a Quarrel (17:1-7)

Rephidim literally means "wide space" in Hebrew. We can't find the location on a map. Ironically, salvation means to "make a wide space," and the people's deliverance leads them to a place in the middle of nowhere. The Israelites have made base camp by traveling in stages, or "zigging and zagging" on their journey.

At this place, the people confront God with a test of whether God will keep God's promises. Moses takes this request personally. "Why do you quarrel with me?" he asks. "Why do you test the LORD?" Moses responds to the Israelites' test by confessing what most leaders do: "I don't know what to do with these people." Moses' leadership arises from vulnerability. Now that the people are faced with unplanned obstacles in their path, Moses realizes that the process of change will not happen overnight.

God responds by reminding Moses and the people that the objects used to deliver them through the sea are also God's instruments to conduct water from rocks in the desert. He processes the elders in front of the people and uses the staff to bring water out of dry ground. "Walk in front of you and take with you some trustworthy things and people," God says. "First of all, take the staff that worked before when you were trying to turn the Nile to blood. It worked before. Now let's see what it can do again." But even more significantly, God says, "Take with you the elders of Israel." The elders play an important role. They become the people who can ask Moses, "What does your faith mean to you in a time of testing? How do you add faith to the equation in a time of water scarcity?"

Why then are the people punished at Rephidim? As we have noticed before, prayer-guing is a common form of communication between God and the people. Surely the issue is not about the media of dialogue but the motive for questioning. Rephidim reveals that the people lacked trust in God to provide for them. Even when the evidence of provision is right before their eyes, the people resist and disobey. The people have already seen God provide water, manna, and quail. By testing God, they demonstrate a lack of faith and a resistance to the Lord's work. The next scene reveals God's battle plan for "unarmed" people.

Armed for Battle (17:8-13)

After God provided water at Massah and Meribah, Amalekites attack the Israelites. This battle is the first time they have been under attack in the wilderness from another people group. Migrating people bump into other people groups. They succumb to a natural tendency to fight with weapons of war and try to destroy one another. War is the default mechanism of most nations. God decides to use this wide place to demonstrate his military prowess. Joshua chooses people to fight with their swords, but they win only because Moses raises his arms to God. Aaron and Hur support his hands, one on one side and one on the other.

Sites of Memory (17:14-16)

At various points along the way, Moses erects monuments to remind the people of the deeds they performed. Obviously, we can't return to these places today. But in Exodus, they're designed to be anchors fixed in the mind so that people can remember God's power and retell the story to future generations. Moses erects a monument at Rephidim called "The LORD is my banner." The altar reminds the people of everything that happened here and the implications going forward in their journey. The Israelites test the Lord; God remains faithful and provides water; and God triumphs over the Amalekites.

Reorganization for the Next Stage (18:1-27)

Just as the Israelites have moved in various stages and have changed, now they need a new way of organizing themselves for the next part of the journey. Moses' strategy as a shepherd will now shift out of the herd mentality and toward his focus as a judge and arbiter of decisions. He will delegate authority to tribal leaders and allow the people to own their choices. Ironically, he learns this lesson from someone who was not an Israelite called out of Egypt. Jethro comes from the tribe of Midian, a religious tribe that follows the "God of Abraham." Moses marries into his family, and God uses Jethro to provide a job for Moses when he's in exile and to continue to mentor Moses at this important moment in his journey.

An Absentee Father (18:1-4)

Chapter 18 opens with a remarkable back story about Moses' relationship with his family. In just a few short verses, we learn about trauma in his wife Zipporah's life. Presumably, the scene at Rephidim has unearthed deep pain in Moses and Zipporah. Often the wilderness will not let us escape the family burdens we carry. Moses has sent his wife and sons away. Recall that this is the same Zipporah who saved Moses' life in Exodus 4. Moses has now cast her aside.

We're not sure why Moses failed as a husband and as a father or chose to lead the Israelites as the absentee father, but we must recognize his shortcomings here and acknowledge that leaders often mask the real struggles they have as parents and spouses. Bad decisions are not lifetime sentences, and Moses' father-in-law intervenes.

A PRESENT PRIEST (18:5-12)

Despite Moses' choices, someone comes out of his past to mentor him and change his management style. Jethro, the Midianite priest, visits Moses and brings Zipporah and their sons with him for reunion and presumably reconciliation. Jethro's background is an important piece to the story of Israel. He's likely a polytheist—a worshiper of many gods. And yet he has seen Yahweh work in the lives of these people, and Moses testifies freely of God's power. Jethro blesses God and goes through a kind of conversion: "Now I know that the LORD is greater than all gods, because he delivered the people from the Egyptians."

Jethro's announcement is remarkable because he is not part of the people who are called out of Egypt. He learns the wonders through testimony and story. He represents other Abrahamic religions—Midianites who see their god through the eyes of Abraham. An ancestor to Arab peoples and followers of Islam today, Jethro is an example of someone who has worshiped the god that he knows from his family. When he encounters the one true God through the witness of Moses, he declares his faith and sacrifices to God. This scene reminds us that God uses all truth to draw people to himself. Jethro's legacy will eventually bear fruit in the lives of other stargazers. The magi of the Christmas story are New Testament astrologers who, like Jethro, go "home by another way" (Matthew 2).

A MANAGEMENT MENTOR (18:13-27)

Jethro not only testifies of God's power but is also an effective administrator. By learning the story of God's power, Jethro also perceives a weakness in Moses—he attempts to lead and manage simultaneously. Moses leads the people in the style of an ancient priest, wanting to represent all of the people's problems to God. He decides to arbitrate each case and make decisions for them. Like he did earlier at Massah and Meribah, Moses has again taken the people's problems on himself and assumes the responsibility to bear their burdens (18:15-16). He selfishly wants power to flow through him. He prefers to wear himself out with the burden of decision making so he can feel as if he's in control of the situations. He is over-functioning and self-sabotaging. He's not gifted at leadership (priest) or management (arbitration), but he also can't let go of the responsibility of either one.

Jethro's wise counsel is like divine intervention for Moses. Jethro counsels Moses to be the priest (leader) and delegate the management and arbitration to tribal leaders. They will serve as judges (18:22). The tribal leaders become fellow burden bearers. In this arrangement, Moses delegates authority and responsibility that he should have never taken on himself. He trains other people to be able to take over if something ever happens to him. Even if the tribal leaders make the wrong decisions, Moses is able to support them and not be responsible for the ongoing struggles of making every decision. Moses' main job is to do the one thing only he can do— remain in tune with God so he can interpret for the people what God wants them to do. Moses will also communicate the people's needs to God. Management and execution of the nation can be handled by detail-oriented people. Moses' other key responsibility is to choose able people to serve over smaller groups. Moses is involved in the difficult cases, but the heads and officers over the people handle the rest.

God's Light in the "Dark Night" of Wilderness

In order to survive, we need the wilderness. Arguably, the Israelites lived better while they were in the wilderness than at any other stage in their history. This landscape rids them of the desires to be in charge and to be self-sufficient; instead, they are fully focused on God and on their role as worshipers and followers.

The scenes in Exodus 17–18 illustrate why. The people test God, and God keeps God's promises despite their resistance. They quarrel, and God moves in their lives. A pagan astrologer converts and demonstrates the power of witness and testimony during a time of deep dependence on God (Exod 18:10-12). Moses is vulnerable, dependent on God to show him when, where, and how to move. He is able to learn, adapt to a new challenge, and delegate authority so the people can survive, so he can endure, and so they can arrive, as Jethro says, "at their home in peace."

The Christian tradition treats the wilderness as a place of tests and salvation. In the Gospels, John the Baptist leads people out to the Jordan River to baptize them—to reenact the wilderness trust in God. Jesus goes into the desert for baptism and conquers evil. For us, it's the place where we learn to rid ourselves of distractions and diversions so we can worship God alone. Wilderness can reveal our deep wounds and long shadows. Like Moses, we confront the painful choices we've made in life, including our regrets and our hurts. Like Zipporah and their children, we also see the miraculous reunions with family that can occur when we never thought they were possible.

John of the Cross was a sixteenth-century mystic who wrote of the "dark night of the soul." We often treat the dark night as a time of distance from God. John of the Cross saw the dark night as precisely the place where we need to be to encounter God.[1] It's the place where we are learning to desire only God and to rid ourselves of other things we want besides union with God. In the wilderness, like the Israelites, we're learning to let go of dependence on self and to be completely dependent on God. John writes that we sense and know God's presence more clearly when we are in a place where we cannot desire anything but God. The dark night is wilderness, a place where God's light shines through unexpected places. We can learn lessons in this place.

1. Wisdom comes from listening to family. In this wilderness place, Moses is able to listen to his father-in-law. He has spent forty years working for him. Now their relationship has changed, and Moses has too.

2. Leadership becomes more effective. Because Moses recognizes his limitations, he is able to delegate effectively and focus on his own responsibilities. Leaders today often think they need to focus on more seminars, learning, techniques, and strategies. These are all important, but they can become gods to distract us from our most important work—differentiating ourselves in our relationship with God. We must learn to focus on the God who rescued us from bondage and hand off the rest to other people. In their responsibilities, they will learn to do the same things. If we are the managers who have been delegated responsibilities, we learn to let the leaders lead and encourage them to be focused on God's vision for the people and on handling big cases.

3. People grow, stretch, and take responsibility. Parents and spouses go through tests of their relationships. We test our children—can you follow my instructions? Our children test us—you said you were going to be home at 5:30, so where have you been? The experience can be a quarrel, a test, or God's victory. The choice in the wilderness is how to respond to the events and how to work with each other in ways that strengthen the bonds we have, confront our shadows, and help us reorganize for the next stage of the journey.

For churches journeying through Covid-19, this season can be a time of testing, renewal, rebirth, or a combination of those. The wilderness of a pandemic teaches us to worship God, trust in daily dependence, and design congregations to be on mission for God in communities where they wander. We can declare "The Lord is my Banner" and reimagine a new way forward through the wilderness together.

I suggest using the tool of asset-mapping during this season. This exercise invites conversation around wilderness questions. For instance, "if there were no staff, facilities, or budget, what would the church still have at its disposal for ministry today?" The church redeploys as God's agents of redemption with new eyes to worship and trust in God.[2]

1. How can the "dark night of the soul" be a positive experience for the believer?

_____

_____

_____

_____

_____

2. Most people have been taught that wilderness is either a transitional phase or a punishment. The book of Exodus treats wilderness as the place of worship. How have your experiences in the wilderness prepared you to worship God?

_____

_____

_____

_____

_____

3. The organizational structure of the Israelites that led them out of bondage did not adequately sustain them in the wilderness. Reflect on your church's journey as a congregation. Is your current organizational structure helping you or holding you back from trust in God?

_____

_____

_____

_____

_____

Notes

1. John of the Cross, *The Collected Works of Saint John of the Cross*, trans. Kieran Kavanaugh and Otilio Rodriguez, rev. ed. (Washington, DC: Institute of Carmelite Studies, 1991), 412.

2. A sample exercise can be found in Cameron Harder, *Discovering the Other: Asset-Based Approaches for Building Community Together* (Herndon, VA: The Alban Institute 2013).

Rules for the Road: How Do We Survive?

Focal Text: Exodus 19:1–24:18

As a student and a pastor, I've had the privilege of attending and leading tour groups. All of them have one thing in common: every group has a set of particular rules for the journey that are written for that organization. It doesn't make sense to give the youth camp rules for the choir tour. The group going to the Holy Land usually doesn't need the same set of rules that a group going to an amusement park needs. The rules are designed for people to enjoy themselves on the journey and to get everyone home safe and sound. Often the rules change and adapt with every trip. By staying within the boundaries as a group, there is freedom to roam and to enjoy. Unless something catastrophic happens beyond the group's control, they will reach their destination and return home without incident. In the case of choir and mission tours, they'll also perform and bear witness to the God who sent them.

The Ten Commandments of Exodus are survival rules for followers of the one true God. These rules reflect a code of conduct that was popular in the ancient world, but they're adapted for the congregations of Israel and the church that follow the living God. It is possible for a person to abide by these rules, live a good life, and be outside the covenant with God. Yahweh offers these rules as a treaty between God and God's people. The commands are not a checklist of duties but rather a living, breathing guide for following God in the wilderness. Simply following the rules doesn't admit a person into the congregation of God's people. God calls and summons us to the mountain to learn with Israel what it means to be constituted as the people of God and to show this worship to others. To use a more modern analogy, the commandments are like a human GPS for pointing and reorienting one's life around the identity given to us at Sinai. They function as a charter for people to be constituted as God's congregation. By listing and abiding by these rules, Israel demonstrates who they are. Their meals, their time, and their laws will indicate who they worship. In this way, the giving of the law is the first "testament" of the people's faith in God and God's faith in them.

The rules function like any other covenant or agreement between two parties in the ancient world. It's a treaty document designed to demonstrate to both sides what it takes to remain in cooperation with each other. At this point in their history, the Israelites have a meal (Passover) and a day (Sabbath). Now God expands on these traditions. God gives them boundaries in order to live well and express themselves to each other. Deliverance out of Egypt is only one part of the redemptive story. God hands Israel a set of laws that become responsibilities to God and to each other. By abiding by these rules, they live.

Preparation to Receive the Law (Exodus 19:1-25)

Before giving them the law, God prepares the people to receive it. He wants worship and fellowship with God's people. God is unique and wants a distinct people for himself. God summons Moses and the people to the mountain to remind them what God has done for them. God makes a commitment to them through a covenant (19:5). If they keep their end of the treaty, God will continue to be faithful to them. Their obedience makes them a "kingdom of priests and a holy nation." This phrase also applies to the church in 1 Peter 2. Their ongoing obedience to the covenant and God's actions in the covenant ratify the agreement (19:1-6).

Moses employs the elders to whom he has delegated responsibility to set these words before the people. The people respond, "All that the LORD has spoken we will do." They consecrate themselves through ritual cleansing and wait for Moses to ascend the mountain. God appears in a smoke-filled theophany that is commonly referred to as the glory of the Lord. God speaks through a thunderous voice in this scene; later we will learn that God speaks to Moses as a friend (19:19; 34:29-35).

God's Top Ten (20:1-21)

God speaks "all these words" that are commonly known as the "Ten Commandments." They are valid in all places and at all times for

God's people and form the frame for applying these words in particular cases in chapter 20. Eventually Jesus uses them as a theme in his
teaching. They begin with a claim of who God is—"I am the LORD
your God who brought you" (Exod 20:2). Because God has saved
the people, God demands of them a certain response. The first four
mandate our commitments to God (vertical); the second six address
our responsibilities to others (horizontal).

1. Have no other gods (v. 3). The first commandment focuses
on God's relationship to and with the deities worshiped by other
cultures. No other god can be in front of or in between God and
God's people. God has an exclusive claim on the people, and God is
the only one the people are to worship.

2. Do not fashion gods (vv. 4-6). The second commandment
describes how humans are to relate to this exclusive deity. God
doesn't want objects made to represent his image. God has made
those images, and they are humans. God's words, "Let us make
humanity in our image," set up the mirror image of God for people
to see and reflect God's character (Gen 1:27). When others see the
character of God's people, they are getting a glimpse into who God
is.

This command comes with a warning and a statement about
God's character that will be revealed more fully when the Israelites
violate this command in Exodus 32. God is jealous. In other words,
like a loving parent, God desires loyalty and will do anything to
contend for his children. Yahweh wants their absolute devotion, and
violation of this command has long-term consequences to future
generations.

3. Take God's name seriously (v. 7). God's name is God's reputation. God's name functions like a brand that the Israelites wear
proudly as a people. Their lives reflect the name, so misuse of that
name either verbally or personally can sully the character of God.
Because the people are images of God, the way they conduct themselves as a people affects God's reputation among other nations. As
Israel goes, so goes God's name.

God's name was not a light thing to ancient Jewish writers. By
the time the Scriptures were beginning to be written, the name of
God evoked fear and awe from scribes. They would come up with
another name for the Lord instead of spelling it out. In fact, when
they came to the place where the name was to be written, ancient
Jewish scribes would clean their pens before writing the name.

4. Remember and keep Sabbath (vv. 9-11). The fourth and fifth commands are framed positively. Just as we learned in the last session, Sabbath was instituted before the people received the law. Time precedes command. There are two parts to the Sabbath law: remember and observe. Both are signified by Sabbath candles today in many Jewish households. They are lit on Friday evening and extinguished Saturday when Sabbath is over.

Sabbath is a remembrance in the way that it takes the people back to the time when God delivered them. Sabbath also *re-members* them. After a fragmented, hurried week, Sabbath puts their lives back together and reconnects them with friends and families. Sabbath is also an observance. They "keep it holy." By ceasing the daily work of life, Sabbath performs maintenance on relationships. The people maintain the tradition, setting it apart as a testimony for all creation. They are to apply it to their lives and to those they supervise and enslave as well. By observing Sabbath, they are able to reflect God's work at creation.

5. Honor your parents (v. 12). The second positive command opens the section on horizontal relationships. This one deals with parental relationships and again is tied to posterity and family lineage. The people live by taking care of parents. In this way, future generations are responsible to their parents rather than the parents feeling like they are the only ones who are taking responsibility for the future. Children prepare for the future by caring for those who brought them into the world.

6. Do not murder (v. 13). Because we are the image of God, and God has called us together out of Egypt, our lives are not ours to destroy. Jesus expands on this teaching and includes motives of the heart as well as hateful words (Matt 5:38). In Israel's case studies, we will learn how this command is applied to those who commit murder. Some, but not all murders, are punishable by death.

7. Do not commit adultery (v. 14). By following God, we are expressing total loyalty to him. Therefore, spousal relationships reflect this loyalty. Since we're bearing the name of the Lord, God's reputation and that of the congregation is damaged when we violate marital oaths.

8. Do not steal (v. 15). Because God will provide what we need, there is no need to take another person's things. We receive what God has given to us and what we have earned fairly from work. We should not take what we haven't been given or what we haven't fairly earned.

9. Do not give false testimony (v. 16). We are not to lie about others. Instead, as Jesus interpreted this passage, we are to let our yes be yes and our no be no (Matt 5:37).

10. Do not covet (v. 17). Because God has given us what we need, what others have is a gift from God as well. We recognize that other people will have more or less than we have. We trust contentedly in what we have so that our desire for another person's possessions does not come between us and God, placing us in violation of the first command.

The people respond to the Ten Commandments in awe and wonder. God follows these commands with instructions on how to erect an altar to him that does not violate the second command (20:18-21).

Case Studies (20:22–23:19)

The covenant now shifts into a list of case studies designed to apply to the Israelite people as they live and worship in the wilderness. As an attorney knows that there is constitutional law and case law, these case studies take the constitution of Israel and apply them to a particular time and place (or case) in their history. We can learn several lessons from these case studies that anticipate an unfolding of God's work later in the people's history.

A JUST COMMUNITY (21:1–22:20)

This section deals with what justice looks like in the wilderness. God addresses what crimes require punishment by death and what crimes do not require punishment. The difference is striking, especially when we compare the wilderness applications to our view of the law today.

Chapters 21–22 addresses seven capital crimes and one non-capital offense.

Capital Crimes
1. Taking a human life, including kidnapping for selling into slavery
2. Dishonoring elders
3. Treating a parent with contempt
4. Female sorcery
5. Bestiality

6. Sacrificing to other gods

7. Injuring a woman in a way that results in her death

Non-capital Offense

Miscarriage or death of an unborn child as a result of injury from another person. Miscarriage is not considered a homicide.

Chapter 22 and the first part of 23 address personal property laws (22:1–23:9). It's striking that people are treated humanely (22:21-27), including resident aliens (23:1-9). Loans are based on poverty and subsistence, not entrepreneurship. God's people do not go into the business of giving someone a loan in order to profit from the transaction. They loan someone money so they can help them get out of a difficult condition. The community benefits when people receive fair treatment while in debt.

God then introduces case law to the Sabbath called the Sabbatical year. The seventh year in the wilderness functions as a time of rest and renewal for workers and property (23:10-19).

An Angel Warrior (23:20-33)

Now that the Israelites have seen God's ability to fight on their behalf against the Amalekites, God announces a new battle plan. An angel warrior will go before the people to drive out enemies who do not fear or worship Yahweh. God's strategy is not to destroy people but to confuse them. He promises to do the fighting for them so they can be peaceful representatives of God's name to others. The right to this land is conditional. By obeying God, they receive the land. They lose the gift through disobedience.

Covenant Ceremony (24:1-18)

The giving of the covenant concludes with a ritual ceremony ratifying the process through the following steps.

1. The covenant is read orally to the people (v. 3). Reflecting the tradition in the ancient world, people heard the word of the Lord spoken to them before this word was ever written down. Rather than Moses having to read God's words silently on a scroll, God speaks to Moses, and Moses speaks the word to the people. The covenant is ratified through oral transmission like an oath pledged at a wedding. By hearing the covenant, the people are constituted.

2. The people respond (v. 3). The call of the covenant elicits the response of the people. They echo the words they said in chapter 19 to start the process, "All the words which the LORD has spoken we will do!"

3. The words are written down (v. 4). After the oral reading and the people's commitment, Moses writes the words down.

4. An altar is constructed (v. 4). Moses erects an altar and twelve pillars. They represent the twelve tribes of Israel and the leaders who have been appointed to assist him with management.

5. They offer a sacrifice (vv. 5-9). They offer a sacrifice of one of the livestock and reread the covenant to the people. The people respond again. They use the blood from the sacrifice to form a blood brotherhood with Moses and the seventy elders. They see the Lord (a rare occurrence in the Scriptures).

6. They eat a meal together (v. 11). They fellowship together in the presence of the Lord, and Moses ascends the mountain to spend forty days and nights with God, receive tablets, and celebrate Sabbath with God. The text suggests that God is still a Sabbath-keeping God even today. Sabbath continues throughout creation.

Living under God's Name with Others

The dramatic scene at Sinai is second only to the Red Sea as the highlight of Exodus. The law begins with a summons and ends with a Sabbath. God eats with his people in fellowship and prescribes rules for their survival. He gives them the freedom and responsibility to live within God's boundaries and promises life for them.

When the Lord sent Jesus, God transferred the name of Yahweh to him, and then Jesus authorized the church to be the bearers of that name as the new Israel. Paul proclaims in Philippians 2 that God has given Jesus a name that is above every name; even in John 17:11, Jesus prayed that God would still protect us by the power of the name.

For those who have grown up in a congregation (a shrinking number in North America), salvation seems to come rather naturally. "Getting saved" is treated as an individual experience. But joining up with the community is a bit more difficult. Salvation is always personal but is never a private affair between me and God. Even when we have a private moment, we are part of a larger community—a group of voices calling out to us, sharing with us, naming us, making us who we are, and showing us whose we are.[1]

These words are expressions of a people who worship the true and living God. That's why we can't understand these as simply etched in granite stone, handed out on a sheet of paper, portrayed on a wall, or emailed around with the instructions, "Just do this." The Ten Commandments are not a "just do it" kind of list. They certainly reflect other moral codes; they do make for better living if people follow them. We forget that one of the reasons people do not follow these words is that step one, to love God, is missing. The words can only be understood as a response to that step—as worship of the living God.

If you're on an airplane, there are certain rules you follow that make sense only at high altitudes. If an oxygen mask drops down from your office ceiling, something is wrong. On an airplane, we know there are oxygen masks in the ceiling. On a cruise ship, the life jacket can be helpful, but we don't need one in everyday life.

In the same way, these commands only make sense when we live them. These laws are not the means by which we enter the community. We don't follow the commands as a checklist to see if we're a Christian or to determine whether we can be baptized. The pattern of Exodus clarifies the process: belonging to the community and believing in God come before behaving. Once we've accepted God's invitation to worship God, then God instructs us how to live.

Every one of these statements about living as the people of God is a road sign and directional marker for how to find our way in life. No matter what situation we're in, the way we discover the next step is to return constantly to these commandments. They orient our lives toward God and others.

When faced with a difficult decision about finances, we go back and reorient our lives to God—worship God above other gods. For in this way the will of God is revealed. As Paul suggests in Romans 12, by living in the way of God, we learn the way God wants us to travel. This is the mystery of the will of God. God does not show the spot on the map, the person we ought to marry, the clothes we should wear, or the car we should drive. With these ten words, God gives us something even more adaptable: the way to make our decisions. The will of God involves living under God's name with God's reputation at stake and following God's commands.

Jesus interprets these words similarly. Instead of merely talking about killing, he applied the words to habits of the heart like anger. Instead of talking about adultery, he dealt with conduct toward people who lust (Matt 5:28). Everything flowed out of real-life situations. If the rules for the road are good enough to point the way, this place called wilderness is good enough for you to take on the road, out the door, and into every part of life.

The Israelites discover that God sets up shop here at Sinai and everywhere else they go. By the time Jesus arrives, he reminds them that the temple was not the sole location of God's presence. Our lives are God's images. Instead, we offer our bodies as living sacrifices every day—whether we are eating cereal, signing in at the hospital, performing surgery, checking the mail, or preparing a meal. When we fellowship at the dinner table and share a plate of food, we are being the people of God.

The law is not the means to enter the community of faith. The law trains the community of faith how to get where we are going. We are able to adapt the laws to fit our situations and contexts because they are deeply interwoven into the fabric of life. They are designed for life itself and adaptable to fit our situations. We can see instances of coveting in every arena of our lives. We can understand that the idea of stealing fits many situations. We can think through killing in so many ways and adapt it to so many situations. These commands are not timebound; they travel from place to place and fit every time and every situation.[2]

God's name is on us, and we have nothing between us and God; honoring God's name becomes paramount to the commands of Exodus. As our lives go, so is God's name reflected and God's reputation enlarged or decreased. We honor God's name through our lips, our lives, and our legacy.

Lips. Our identity as God's covenant people makes us care what's on our lips. Does what we say reflect the majesty of God's name? When we make a promise, do we keep it? When we say God's name, do we mean it? When we get angry, do we say things that are worthy of that name on our lives? Jesus knew something that the Pharisees didn't. It's not what we consume through our mouths that affects our lives; it's what comes out of our mouths, which is rooted in the heart and mind, that matters (Matt 12:34). For example, in Acts 5, Ananias and Sapphira withheld their money from the treasury of the church and still claimed they were giving their all for God. Peter promptly showed them and the church (sending shock waves everywhere) that God's name is important. If you're going to carry it around, you certainly can't lie about your contributions to the church. Those two people died on the spot.

Lives. When we take God's name seriously, it affects our lives. As we noted before, Jesus says that what is on your lips is also a walking billboard for your life. To miss out on opportunities, to waste moments that could be used for him, to slack off is taking God's name in vain. Jesus says later in his great sermon that he encountered all kinds of people who would say, "Lord, Lord." But what did he say about them? "Not everyone who says to me 'Lord, Lord' will enter heaven but only he who does my father's will" (Matt 7:21). If we simply believe and say "Lord, Lord" but are not truly living as God wants us to, we are taking God's name in vain. The worst blasphemy we can ever commit, as Elton Trueblood has said, is not a word of profanity but of lip service to the Lord.[3]

Legacy. When we take the Lord's name seriously, others take us seriously. The cure for apathy today is taking God's name that he has given us so seriously in our lives that people will care enough to live as we do. In this way, we will find ourselves leaving behind a lasting legacy of commitment to that name.

1. The Ten Commandments (or words) are the way God preserves God's people. How do these laws provide life to you today?

_____

_____

_____

_____

_____

2. The people celebrate the giving of the law, and God keeps Sabbath and fellowships with Moses. How do you demonstrate fellowship and joy in the midst of obedience?

_____

_____

_____

_____

_____

3. God calls the people before giving them rules. Belonging as a covenant people and believing in God precede behaving correctly. How does this process change your view of the church? What part of the process does your church emphasize? How can belonging become just as important as behaving?

_____

_____

_____

_____

_____

Notes

1. See Eugene Peterson, *Christ Plays in Ten Thousand Places: A Conversation in Spiritual Theology* (Grand Rapids: Eerdmans, 2008), 253.

2. Terence Fretheim, *Exodus*, Interpretation (Louisville: John Knox, 1991), 223.

3. Elton Trueblood, *Foundations for Reconstruction* (Waco: Word Books, 1972), 31.

Part 4

The Destination: God's Presence with Us

(Exodus 25:1–40:30)

Designing a Place: Where Will God Meet with Us?

Exodus 25:1–31:17

People who work for political candidates and performing artists share something in common: they would not have a job without the election or tour. They can't work unless the artist performs or the candidate runs. The candidates and the artists can't do their work of speaking and performing without a team going ahead of them, preparing a place, gathering the people, and selling tickets. An effective campaign or tour requires the team as well as the leader.

If celebrities require that much preparation before they arrive at a place, imagine the significance of the tabernacle scenes in Exodus. God wants to have a place to meet with God's people along the way. God has called, delivered, and constituted the Israelites. Now God designs a place to meet the pilgrims as they journey. God does not intend to remain on the mountain. Like a traveling artist, God moves and continues to do so. But now that God has a people to represent God, God wants to check in with them, cleanse the people's sins, dwell with the people, and rest among them.

In order to have a place for gathering and fellowship, God follows a pattern similar to the one outlined in the seven days of creation in Genesis. In this session we will see several themes that remind us of the creation account in Genesis 1. As Terence Fretheim notes, God speaks seven times in chapters 25–31, signifying the seven days of creation.[1] The seven candlesticks of the lampstand are reminiscent of the seven days of creation. God instructs Aaron to light the lamp of the lampstand with the same words from Genesis 1: "Let there be light." This design section ends the way the first seven days of creation conclude—with a Sabbath. God allocates an offering, designs a mobile chest and tent, provides instructions for the meeting, appoints the ministers, and empowers the workers.

On the journey from Egypt to the promised land, God makes provisions so that the Israelites will always know where to meet God when God arrives. God is working, moving, and active. God had planned to come and go at will, but the Hebrews need the reassurance that when God arrives, they have a place for God to rest. This mobile pavilion known as the tabernacle serves as a meeting place, worship center, treaty holder, and commander's outpost for the band of pilgrims. The place doesn't have to be pretty; it simply has to be prepared according to God's specifications. This is God's place for God to meet them when God arrives. Like an advance team for a performing artist who is contracted to do the work, Israelites prepare a facility so that when God arrives in their midst, they are ready to respond. The ark contains tablets certifying they had a right to be the people for this God and prepare this place for God.

God is reassuring the people that regular meetings on the journey will be a part of their lives with God. They receive a plan that forms and shapes their identity. Even as they wander, whether as Israelites on a journey to the promised land or as a church in exile, they can rely on the pattern God provides in the wilderness and be assured that God will meet with them. They recognize their role in God's recreated meeting place. God uses all of the Israelites' skills and abilities, and the priests serve God on the journey. The tabernacle scenes explain how Jesus' work as high priest takes on even deeper meaning. They expand our understanding of God's cosmic effect on the world.

God's Offerings (25:1-7)

The creation of an earthly space begins when God institutes a voluntary offering ("from all whose hearts prompt them to give," v. 2). The people's gifts are a part of the design process, and their gifts come from their work and talents. God lists the supplies separately so each tribe and household can choose which part fits their house. In other words, the textile makers, metal workers, leather makers, woodworkers, olive dressers, and incense makers give gifts of textiles, precious metals, leather, wood, oil, incense, and spices respectively, according to their trades.

God's Blueprint (25:8–27:21)

With the plans for the capital campaign set prior to construction, God reveals what the people will erect on the journey. Remarkably, these scenes recall God's instructions to Noah for building the ark in Genesis. God issues designs, and Noah constructs a space to preserve God's people, transport them through a storm, and reconstitute them when the disaster is over. In the case of the tabernacle, the people have already been saved and are on the journey to the new destination. God involves them in a similar exercise as the one Noah performed.

The instructions in this section move functionally and practically from the most holy objects and spaces in the center of the tabernacle, outward to the less holy spaces until they reach the exterior courtyard. Since the purpose is primarily to meet with God and to perform the requisite meeting rituals, the focus is on the furniture and the form of the space that will inform the functions. Little is mentioned here about the actual sacrifices; the book of Leviticus provides those details. Exodus is shaped around God's visual pattern, anchoring these designs into the people's collective memory so that whenever and wherever they want to gather to meet God, they will remember how to assemble a space and prepare their community. The process of remembering the design and preparing their lives is the actual process of convening for God's presence. Exodus teaches us that by going through the process, we invite God's presence to dwell with us.

THE ARK (25:10-16)

Like Noah's ark, the centerpiece of the meeting is another ark made from the same materials as Noah's—acacia wood, but this time the size of a carrying trunk. Converted to the imperial system of measurement, the ark is 3.75 feet long, 2.25 feet deep, and 2.25 feet wide. Covered with gold inside and out, the ark is designed to be portable, carried from the bottom using large poles. The ark contains the tablets ("testimony" in most English versions) that God will give to them. The tablets include the valid contract that God inscribes, signifying that God has entrusted God's name and reputation in the world to these people. They have been called out of Egypt to show others who God is and to demonstrate through their pilgrimage and behavior that God is Lord above all other gods. The tablets are a treaty document that God writes. These charter stones present to other tribes who the Israelites are and explain what constitutes them as a people. Without them, they are classified as "Hebrews"—a word that in the ancient near east could mean "fugitive," "peasant," or "outlaw."[2] But now, with these tablets—literally God's testimony about them to others—they have an identity and a mission. Just as God protected the handful of people through the flood to save them from themselves, now God designs another ark to preserve God's witness about a relatively small group of people and to identify who they are to other tribes.

THE MERCY SEAT (25:17-22)

The ark's cover includes two winged cherubim facing one another and molded from the same gold as the rest of the ark. This is the place where God will meet with the people and is called the mercy seat. Because God convenes meetings with the people, God also wants to show them mercy and continue a relationship with them. This mercy seat reminds the people of God's kindness toward them by providing the tablets as instructions on what to do. There is not a focus on the past burden of guilt. God moves with them from this place. By giving them tablets and meeting with them, he shows mercy. By agreeing to meet with them on the journey, God allows the people to atone for the their sins and gives them commands to keep them clean, safe, and alive (25:22).

Although Leviticus emphasizes the significance of blood as a cleanser, Exodus places just as much importance on the act of meeting with God. When we claim that Jesus "covers our sins," we also declare that God meets with us (1 John 1:7). God's presence dwells incarnationally with us in the person of Jesus. That process begins in the wilderness (Heb 9:1-28).

THE TABLE (25:23-30)

The table in front of the ark is relatively small. Shaped like an ottoman, the table is 3 feet long and only 1.5 feet wide and tall. The table too is made of acacia wood overlaid with gold. The table has room for gold plates, dishes, bowls, and fellowship bread. Since we learn later that God refreshes himself on the Sabbath, the bread suggests that this is the people's way of sharing a meal with God. When God meets, God likes to eat! (See Exodus 24:11, where the men fellowshipped with God on the mountain.)

THE LAMP WITHOUT OIL (25:31-40)

To prepare for a priest to light the lamp, God places a seven-stem lampstand in the room. The menorah, which will eventually become an important symbol used in Hanukkah celebrations, signifies the seven days of creation. It contains a center trunk with almond branches flowering with buds and blossoms.

THE TABERNACLE (26:1-30; COMPARE 36:20-34)

The tabernacle functions like a portable garrison for a traveling commanding officer on the battlefield. The tabernacle also previews the dimensions and architecture of Solomon's temple. Exodus indicates that this is the place where God will meet with God's people when God is present with them. They will perform for God the various necessary sacrifices. The aesthetic attention to detail indicates that beauty and holiness go together. God will atone for their sins and give them instructions for the next stage of the journey. Their representatives—the priests—will prepare a message to God on their behalf, and the priests will be vested with signs of their office and a connection to God.

Ironically, however, with all of its details, the blueprint does not reveal how precisely to fit the structure together or the exact thickness of the frames. No one is completely sure of its size and shape, but biblical scholars agree that the tabernacle was forty-five feet long, fifteen feet wide, and fifteen feet tall. The altar was on the west end, and the entrance was on the east. The two outer coverings were tanned ram skins and another inexpensive animal skin, and the two inner layers were fabric. The exterior was dyed red. The fabric was dyed either blue, purple, or crimson. Although many attempts are made to see some christological significance in the colors of the fabrics, no suggestion of this is made in Exodus, Hebrews, or any other New Testament writing.

What is clearer is that costlier fabrics and metals are reserved for the holiest spaces. Once the tabernacle is assembled, God will continue to meet with the people, make decisions, and give them instructions. The people will be saved from themselves and disaster. God will accept the sacrifices that are offered and inform the priest of God's decisions. They are to construct a place for these acts to be performed.

THE HOLY OF HOLIES (26:31-37)

The inner chamber, the holy place or holy of holies, will be behind a veil, a fabric partition inscribed with cherubim. The outer entrance has a fabric screen without the cherubim. The inner veil does have important New Testament significance in Matthew 27 and Hebrews

9. Our lives are tied intimately to what Jesus is doing behind the veil and continues to do on our behalf.

The death of Jesus helps us understand the significant work of what was going on at the tabernacle and the continual work that Jesus does on our behalf now. It tells us the origins of how Jesus wants to meet with us. When Aaron meets the Lord, God's presence is always outside the box the people have made for him. God's presence is always bigger than we imagine. Jesus goes behind the curtain that separates the high priest from the people and offers his life as the sacrifice for the people. As Tom Long suggests, we don't cure the sin problem with more information. We cure the sin problem with Christ's continual work and with our continual growth, change, and development. The same goes for a church.[3]

C. S. Lewis captures this sense in *The Lion, the Witch and the Wardrobe*—there is something going on in the supernatural realm that makes this world possible, not the other way around. The children arrive in Narnia realizing that they thought their world was the only one. But suddenly a whole other world exists, waiting to be explored. Like the children, we need training to see this world; and interestingly enough, that's the world we are headed into one day and are rehearsing now on the journey.[4]

The tabernacle scenes also suggest to us that God has a plan. As much as we have access to God, we also know that we don't have the full plan. There is something yet to be revealed. We do have a part to play in the construction, design, setup, and teardown. And we're all involved in that process.

THE ALTAR AND COURTYARD (27:1-19)

Outside the holiest places, we see a design for a massive hollow wooden altar covered with bronze and with a bronze grill inside. The emphasis is on the size and symbolism, not the function. Measuring 7.5 feet long, 7.5 feet wide, and 4.5 feet tall, the altar describes but does not prescribe the kinds of sacrifices that will be given there. If this altar is portable, the people will have some heavy lifting to do! The bronze metal suggests that the ongoing sacrifices will be offered here, in a space less sacred than the holiest places that are covered with gold and costly fabrics. (The text does not turn to the instructions about the offerings themselves until Exodus 29:38–30:10, when the priests are given their instructions.) Surrounding the altar is a large courtyard 150 feet long and 75 feet wide. The screen curtains are as high as the altar—or 7.5 feet tall.

THE OIL FOR LIGHT (27:20-21; SEE ALSO 30:22-38)

God's first word in Genesis was "Let there be light." To signify the creation of a meeting place, God lights the darkness. This passage connects to the seven days of creation and to the recreation of the world after the flood. The text returns to the lamp behind the tent and the oil required to light the lamp. The emphasis is on the offering of the people (the pure oil) and the appointment of Aaron and his sons as priests to tend the lamp. With the courtyard in place, God says, "Let there be light."

God's Priests (28:1–29:46)

CLOTHING (28:1-43)

God commissions Aaron and his sons to serve God (not the people) as a priestly family. Meeting in God's presence is holy work in a sacred space. The priest bears the burden of the people's sins as well as the responsibility of God's judgments and decisions. What does a priest wear when he meets with God inside the tent? These clothes matter because they represent the people to God. The priest serves God, but the people are always on his body. There are seven articles of clothing that have special significance: ephod, breastpiece, robe, tunic, turban, sash, and undergarments.

We don't know what an ephod is, but we do know that the garment represents the persons and tribes associated with Israel. The breastpiece represents the judgments and decisions that God makes in the presence of the priest. The stones on the breastpiece bear the names of the sons of Israel. Inside the breast pocket, near the heart, is another pair of stones (like dice) called the Urim and the Thummim (28:30). God uses chance to carry out God's will. God hasn't predetermined every step we or even God will take. God's will allows freedom of choice and surprises along the way. Aaron carries those instruments of chance with him.

Priestly work is dangerous business and carries with it the potential of death if the rituals are not performed correctly. God wants to keep the priests alive, so God allows them to wear bells to ring in God's presence and to prevent death. God cares about what happens to the priests. According to Brueggemann, "the priests had better get it right with the bells" (28:35).[5] If they make a mistake, they will die in God's presence.

The priests wear a turban with the phrase "Holy to the Lord" inscribed on a rosette fastened to the turban (28:36). Aaron's work with the people is intimately bound with the people represented in his clothing. The tunic and sash are aesthetically pleasing; the undergarments are designed to cover the priest's nakedness.

Ordaining (29:1-37)

The clothes worn by the priests symbolize the people and the purpose of God's meeting. The people do not choose the priests, and their successors inherit their role. In order to maintain the integrity of the priestly order, the people perform a seven-day sacred ritual (29:35) that echoes the seven days of creation and focuses on the person of the priest rather than his function. In other words, God focuses more on the character of the person and the relationship with that person than the competencies and functions of the job. God is less concerned at this point with the meeting rituals (liturgy, administration, and delegation). God seems to be concerned about the person's education, background, or qualifications for the job. In this first ordination ceremony, God focuses on character formation, relationship of the person to God and the relationship of the person to the people. Only the priest and the people can hold each other accountable. The ordination rituals highlight these roles.

The Hebrew word "to ordain" means literally "to fill the hand" (29:9). The people are entrusting their lives to Aaron, the sacrificial rites, and the responsibility of meeting with God. Aaron in turn places his hands on the sacrificial bull. The people use a sacrificial ram, its blood, and its guts to symbolize the intimate connection among the people, the blood, and the holiness of the priest. This act is a precursor to the ordination process of laying hands on the head of the one being ordained (29:15). In verse 24, the people place on Aaron's and his sons' palms the blood from the guts of the ram. The priests in turn literally wave the ram's breast before the Lord and the people as an offering (29:26-28).

Purpose of Ordination and Sacrificial Performances (29:42-46)

The last few verses of chapter 29 recap why ordination rituals are important and preview the construction of the altar in chapter 30. Why do we need a sacrificial process? Because God wants to meet us, associate with us publicly, and give us an identity. Presence and meeting intersect. The regular burnt offering reminds the people that God wants to meet, speak, and abide with them. The implication is that God wants to dwell among them but cannot do so in the land of Egypt. God wants to "hang out." God desires for them to know who brought them out and who is their Lord and God. Presence, assembly, and identity come together. With God's presence, our gathering, and God's consecration, we are able to know that we are God's people. Our identity in Christ isn't something we're born with; it's something that God calls us to by meeting with us, informing us who we are, and reminding us who God is. We reconstitute our identity with God and God's identity with us every time we gather in his presence.

The Altar, Incense, Atonement Tax, and Completion (30:1–31:18)

The altar is placed outside the holiest place, and Aaron offers incense there daily. The altar previews the ways our lives are offered as a fragrant aroma to God (2 Cor 2:15). The people smell the fragrance every day.

The people's membership in the covenant community is confirmed annually with an atonement tax derived from a counting method literally called "to raise the heads." They count heads and base their offering for their annual membership in the community and in atonement for their sins. All of their lives—money included—are a sacred offering. The priests also use a basin for washing. This section contains the recipes for the anointing oil and incense (30:22-38). It's unlikely that these ingredients could have been found on a pilgrimage through the desert. As this section indicates, God "shows the pattern." This section is written as the recipe for a time when the people are able to locate the ingredients.

GOD'S SPIRIT FALLS ON THE PEOPLE (31:1-11)

God appoints a priestly family to serve God. They inherit their jobs through the generations. God's Spirit appoints craftspeople to serve not through biology but through gifts and abilities. God anticipates people to build the space through God's spirit. When God's Spirit first falls on a person, it does so on two craftsmen named Bezalel and Oholiab. We will meet them again in the construction of the tabernacle. The Spirit's presence is alive and well on the people as much as on the priests. There is no distinction in God's work between clergy and laity. The priests serve God, and the architects carry out the mission of the Spirit. Both are necessary in order for the people to meet in God's presence and for God to dwell with the people. Before Moses leaves the mountain, God identifies people to serve in these capacities.

God's Refreshment of Time and Place (31:12-18)

If God journeys with us, we're going to need to acknowledge that God needs rest from us. Just as the seventh day of creation is designed for God to rest, so the Sabbath in the wilderness is designed for God to refresh himself (31:17). The Israelites keep the Sabbath as a sign of their treaty agreement and identity with God. The world knows that these people worship Yahweh as Lord because they keep a Sabbath on the seventh day. It's such a sacred day that violation of the Sabbath law and failure to get enough rest is punishable by death. Presumably this is why many Israelites died in Egypt—because they could never take a day off. They certainly did not have a concept of a weekend. But the other reason to keep the Sabbath is to give God a chance to have rest. Even God needs a day off. This section concludes with the "finger of God" on the tablets/testimony that will be placed in the ark when Moses descends from the mountain. We can already sense the drama of what is to come.

Act 2 of a Cosmic Narrative

The creation of the world through the covenant with Abraham, Isaac, and Jacob is Act 1 of a sacred drama in Scripture. Exodus is Act 2. By creating a meeting place for God, the tabernacle fills in a missing piece of Israel's history in Egypt. Without a Sabbath or a space in Egypt, there was no time or place for meetings. The people were exhausted and dying, and so was the memory of the one true God. By calling them out of Egypt and giving them commandments, God allows the people to live again. God wants to be a part of this adventurous journey with presence, and he provides priests and architects to serve him and build the space. The people participate with their talents, money, and time to build the mobile fellowship and atonement space. They lay the groundwork for the significant work that Jesus will fulfill through his death on the cross.

The book of Hebrews expands on the blueprints that are revealed in Exodus. God shows the pattern, and Hebrews takes that pattern and reveals another dimension to God's cosmic architecture. Deeply influenced by Platonic thinking, the audience of Hebrews assumes that they are trapped in a world with only shadows of visible truth (Heb 9:1-5; 10:1-2). Using categories God's audience would understand, the preacher of Hebrews casts the tabernacle rituals as a Platonic foreshadowing of a Christ who descends to us and brings light, truth, and hope into our world. Hebrews suggests that the Israelites were stuck in a cave looking at shadows of the true forms above (Heb 9:11-28).

Today, we are not looking at shadows, but most people know that something is not right with the world. Something is going on "out there" that makes us feel massively out of control; or someone is controlling something out there that makes it impossible for us to get out of the circumstances we're in. The people on the top are always on the take, and we're stuck helpless in a trap.

As I have learned from my preaching students, African American families migrated north and west in the early twentieth century to escape the Jim Crow South, terror, and lynching. However, in many cities throughout the country—north and south—struggles are ongoing to survive in the face of police brutality, gun violence, mass incarceration, and systemic poverty, leaving too many people in our country feeling helpless and trapped. The recent murders of Ahmoud Arbery, George Floyd, and Breonna Taylor have re-awakened the country to the plight of Black Americans. We have also watched helplessly as communities have faced overwhelming militaristic police presence as well as rioting. The retired African American police chief David Dorn was murdered in the midst of looting.

Exodus speaks to those who feel stuck, but the solution doesn't come through the sacrifice of bulls and rams. The blueprints God reveals on the mountain are fulfilled in ways that the pilgrim people could understand and participate in. The book of Hebrews takes the same blueprints and shows how Jesus Christ's work fits the pattern. In other words, just as Jesus fulfilled what the Israelites first experienced, there is no Christian experience of Jesus without the architecture from Exodus (Hebrews 3–11).

What is that pattern? After creation, Exodus functions as an important second act in the biblical drama that culminates in Jesus' work and continues through the church today. God is not waiting for liberation; he's coming to us in our circumstances. Jesus is breaking through the barriers of the world and coming to us (Heb 10:5-10).

To motivate people the way the New Testament book of Hebrews does, it's necessary to involve them in the design journey. We can't understand who we are or why we are here without pulling out the blueprints of our church and of our lives that God had for us all along. By understanding the past, we're able to live into the present work of God.

Exodus and Hebrews do more than just reveal a blueprint. The preacher of Hebrews acknowledges the flaws in the system that created corruption. The priestly families of yesterday and today are flawed characters (Heb 11:23-28). Clergy are prone to wander. So, as Hebrews 9:15 says, Christ becomes the sacrifice and goes to the altar for us. He steps in and functions as the executor of the estate. Whereas human clergy—Israelite or Christian—could never fully accomplish what the chief architect wanted, Jesus accomplishes everything for us and with us.

> Therefore he is the mediator of the new covenant, so that those who are called may receive the promised eternal inheritance, since a death has occurred which redeems them from the transgressions under the first covenant. For where a will is involved the death of the one must be established. (Heb 9:15)

Jesus' death makes it possible for a new agreement to be signed. He's not only the one who has died but also the executor who calls us, pleads with us, and begs us to claim that inheritance as our own. Just as his work fulfills the blueprint's design, his death becomes like the reading of a will, an inheritance that we receive in forgiveness. In other words, his death is the tablet/testimony that we need. If we want to know if God has a peace treaty with us, we can look at the tablets inscribed by the finger of God. They point to his son who has died on the cross for us. God demonstrates now his commitment to us. The covenant agreement becomes a first edition of a last will and testament from God to us. The first set of tablets is a gift to us.

Conclusion

The Israelites are on a journey to become a new people with little direction on how long this will take. With an eye toward the future temple that one day will be built in Jerusalem, God summons Moses along with Aaron and his sons. They have a design conversation about the construction of a mobile tabernacle and the attendants required to worship and serve God. In the process of designing the tabernacle, God also reveals the process needed to prepare pilgrim people for following God through the wilderness and into the new territory that God has given them. God uses the design process to prepare people as much as the building and construction itself. The passage does not teach us how to design a capital campaign, but we are suggesting that the rehearsal, planning, and thinking necessary for the journey ahead can be just as significant as the journey itself. Designing can be a sign and a symbol of what the journey will be like. By getting Moses and Aaron and his sons involved, God sends a strong signal that this tabernacle is not merely dictated from the sky but that the people will need to be prepared before they move into the new world that God has given them.

For the church today, Exodus teaches us how to treat God when we're in the wilderness journey. In other words, when a church is in the process of being reborn and recreated, we need to remember six things.

1. What God went through to meet with us. It's one thing for us to remember the past by looking to see what other people went through. It's another thing to remember what God had to go through in order to meet us. This is how trapped, busy, distracted, and enslaved we were. God had to deliver the people out of bondage, only to discover that they quarreled against each other, tested God, and disobeyed.

2. Ordained clergy serve God first. We "fill their hands" with expectations and responsibilities, but their primary work is to serve God. Evaluate clergy on their character as much as their competence. God ordains Aaron not because he is a great strategist or manager but because he can appear in God's presence with spiritual sacrifices ready to meet God. Today's churches should be more interested in the depth of spiritual character and growth of the pastor. Encourage the pastor to serve the Lord first; the work of the people will flow out of that work of character.

3. Time and space matter. As a tabernacle people, we need to pause in our schedules, come together, and create temporary dwelling places and structures so that God can rest. Sabbath keeping and congregating are the witness to the world that there is a one, true, holy God.

4. God ratified a treaty with us long before Jesus came. Jesus doesn't replace the tablets; he's the architect behind the blueprints. He does what earthly priests and wilderness sacrifices were never designed to do. He is both the designer and the priest. He dwells with us as God's glory and designs the pattern that we follow today. By worshiping Jesus, we are worshiping God's priest and designer. He provides another part of the blueprints that a wandering people could have never imagined—Gentiles and Jews equally inheriting what wandering Israelites already received: a way to meet, fellowship, and gather with a God who wants to dwell with them.

5. God's focus is on holy meeting places and times. We can imagine that in Exodus, God says something like, "Just as I'm different from you, so is the time and space set apart for me to meet with you. I'm planning to come down the mountain with you and in the people— here's how I want you to think about me."

6. God wants to spend time with us publicly. Just as God preserved the people in an ark, he wants to be with us as we wander. God wants to rest, renew, and fellowship with us.

1. There is a difference between a mobile tabernacle and a permanent temple. How does your church participate in tabernacle faith? How can your congregational life feel more like a pilgrimage and less like a destination?

_____

_____

_____

_____

_____

2. How does the design process of the tabernacle become formative for the life of the congregation? Who are the designers in your church that need affirmation for their imagination and planning?

_____

_____

_____

_____

_____

3. How can the demands of congregational life prevent ministers from serving God? How do you "fill their hands" so they can serve God more faithfully?

_____

_____

_____

_____

_____

Notes

1. Terence Fretheim, *Exodus*, Interpretation (Louisville: John Knox, 1991), 270.

2. Niels Peter Lemche, "Hebrew," *ABD* 3:95.

3. Thomas Long, *Preaching from Memory to Hope* (Louisville: Westminster John Knox Press, 2009), 9.

4. C. S. Lewis, *The Lion, the Witch, and the Wardrobe* (New York: HarperCollins, 1994).

5. Walter Brueggemann, "Exodus," in *General Articles on the Old Testament, the Book of Genesis, the Book of Exodus, the Book of Leviticus*, vol. 1 of New Interpreter's Bible (Nashville: Abingdon, 1994), 912.

Face to Face:
Why Is God So Angry?

Focal Text: Exodus 32:1–34:35

Between the design and construction of the tabernacle, Exodus reveals yet another dimension to the character of the Israelites, their leaders Moses and Aaron, and the God that they follow. The Israelites are deeply flawed, impatient people who apostatize by making a bull idol to worship Yahweh. They violate the first command given at Sinai. Aaron, recently installed as priest, instigates the treason and attempts to triangulate the people against God and Moses. God and Moses wrestle over the right thing to do with the people and argumentatively resolve to move forward together with most of the people who came from Egypt. It's a remarkable scene of recreation, restoration, and redemption. This session examines how the "golden calf" experience reveals who these characters are at their core. As in any family system, we don't understand a person until we see them struggle with their shadow side and stretch to remain loyal in the midst of betrayal. What we see on social media platforms like Facebook is only a small picture of a person's life. In the case of biblical characters, their stories are incomplete without their struggles and failures, even where God questions God's own decisions to save them. But this is the whole gospel, and it is also the story of life.

No one ever tells you what is truly involved in parenting ahead of time. You learn as you go. The same can be said of most positions in work and church. We love the call of God, and we also learn the realities of working with people. It is only by ministering, dialoguing, and working through the challenges that a walk with God can be truly understood. It is through these challenges that we are able to see God and the people for who they are—to come face to face with reality. In the process, like Moses, we learn to talk with God as a friend.

Consequences of Worshiping God the Wrong Way (32:1-35)

A Substitute for Delayed Instructions (32:1-6)

Moses is on the mountain receiving the tablets from God. While the people wait below for the next steps, they anxiously ask Aaron to do something so they can worship God. Their request is ambiguous, suggesting they're not even sure what they want. "Come, make a god/gods for us," they say. The expedient invitation, the ambiguity of the request, and Aaron's response indicate that the people are not attempting to apostatize at first; they want to create something tangible to represent their worship of Yahweh.

Aaron responds by demanding an offering of precious jewels that he quickly casts into an image of a bull, the fertility god common in the ancient Near East. He proclaims a festival *to Yahweh* (32:5) with the calf as the totem, and the people celebrate God with an object they created.

The opening scene with the golden calf brings into sharp relief a distinctive of following God. Idolatry is not simply worshiping multiple gods other than Yahweh. Idolatry (and apostasy) is tantamount to using anything to substitute for God's presence. The Sinai command "You shall have no other gods before me" is another way of saying "You shall have nothing else in front of my face" or "You shall have nothing else as a substitute for my presence or as a mediator of my presence to you." The people disobey not because they fail to worship Yahweh. They choose to worship God the wrong way.

"Prayerguing" with God (32:7-14)

While the people celebrate, God turns into an angry parent ready to abandon his children. God informs Moses that *Moses'* people (not God's) have apostatized (32:7). Operating from negative emotions, God burns with hot anger and attempts to disassociate himself from them and accuses them of being stiff-necked or obdurate. This charge is the ultimate sign of infidelity—they have behaved as the pharaoh did when he refused to let the people go. From God's perspective, the people have enslaved themselves. Like an angry parent who probably knows he needs to calm down, God grieves the next steps. God says "let me alone" so that God can stew over the problem.

Moses responds by not letting God withdraw from the conversation. He offers another prayer-argument or "prayergument" with

God. He treats God not like the angry parent but as the merciful patient judge that God is. Like Abraham pleading for Sodom, Moses wants God to act in God's best interests. Instead of using emotional appeals, he uses logical evidence to remind God of God's commitments to the people. Instead of grounding his prayer in the people's actions, he bases his appeal on God's character. God does not excuse Israel's behavior; Moses reminds God of his commitments in spite of that behavior. Moses reminds God of the people's identity in God (32:11); God's reputation among the Egyptians (32:12); and the covenant oath with Abraham, Isaac, and Jacob (32:13). God's anger cools, and he changes his mind.

Moses' prayer is based on the ancient practice of recollection. Prayer functions not only as a request for deliverance but also as a reminder to God of the commitments God has already made to himself and the people. By recalling God's promises, the people learn who God is and grow more faithful to the God who calls them. The people follow God not because they are perfect or forgiven but because God is faithful to keep God's promises to them.

TRIANGULATING AARON AND THE PEOPLE (32:15-24)

Following an angry encounter with God, Moses channels God's anger toward the people. Ironically, he does not leave the tablets with God; he brings them down the mountain to the people in a symbolic display of covenant breaking. In this scene, God is only present through the tablets. Moses seizes the situation, and God is speechless. Moses burns with hot anger and shifts the blame to Aaron. In turn, Aaron states that he is a victim of the people's demands. He says he merely required the offering, but the calf "magically" appeared out of the fire.

God and Moses respond similarly. Both of their reputations are at stake, and their first response is hot anger that burns jealously for their relationship with the people and their survival. Unfortunately, hot anger rarely results in redemptive action. It's usually a short-term reaction based on immediate circumstances. Another response to infidelity—cool anger—recognizes the damage inflicted by the person but understands the need for a long-term solution that restores the relationship as best as possible and preserves the life of the person. Before his anger gets the best of him, Moses gives the people a chance to choose loyalty.[1]

INVITATION TO FIDELITY (32:25-35)

In order to forestall the coming consequences, and in an effort to give the people one more chance, Moses calls the people to account. Their wild behavior can be attributed to Aaron, and Moses recognizes that recommitment can solve the problem. In a scene that previews the opening of the book of Joshua, Moses calls people to recommit to fidelity to God. Loyalty covers a multitude of wild behaviors. Remarkably, most choose to remain on Aaron's side. A Levite family preserved Moses' life in a basket in the Nile River (Exod 2:1-10). Now members of the same tribe become standard bearers of holiness. Their significant role in the history of Israel emerges in the midst of apostasy. They saved Moses from Pharaoh; now they save Israel from sabotage. Their first task is to cleanse the camp of anyone who threatens their survival. By stepping forward in faithfulness to Moses and God, they "ordain" themselves. Just as the people ordained Aaron earlier in Exodus, now the Levites self-ordain through surrender and service to the Lord and thereby bless themselves.

Following the Levites' slaughter, there is still sin that needs to be atoned. Moses approaches God again like a priest on behalf of his people. He offers to make atonement or "cover" for their sin by exchanging his name in God's book for theirs. This story previews the eventual formal tradition of ancient Judaism: on the day of atonement, people would offer their sacrifice at the temple, and their families' names would be entered into God's book for a year. Moses functions as a burden bearer for the people before God. Whatever punishment they are to face, he wants to cover the cost with his own life. Like a parent willing to pay for damages caused by a child's reckless behavior, Moses wants to do whatever it takes to keep God's children with God.

God rejects Moses' offer to cover their sin, but eventually God shows mercy and forgives. In the meantime, God promises an eventual punishment. Verse 35 says that God "strikes the people" (the NAS reflects the Hebrew words, not the use of "plague" as in the NRSV), completing the necessary punishment to move forward. The text places blame at the feet of Aaron for enabling infidelity.

Was all of this slaughter necessary? From our perspective, of course not. This is not an example story for church discipline. But it's also just as likely that the people would have continued to self-sabotage while Moses led the erection of the tabernacle. Most construction managers have been through mutiny or insurrection.

In the Israelites' case, by refusing to follow Moses, they self-select death and punishment.

The point of this scene is not to offer a universal norm for the ways God interacts with us—or the ways we interact with each other. No one is appointed as Levites today to slaughter people. Instead, the Bible lays bare the deep-seated deception and betrayal that are often endemic to leadership and community building. This passage effectively demonstrates the human condition and the complexities of leadership. Even the God we serve responds angrily and also redemptively. God changes God's mind because of effective prayer and dialogue.

Going with God's Presence (33:1-23)

PREPARING TO GO (33:1-6)

Following the punishment, God announces an astonishing decision. God wants the people to go on the trip without him. Like a parent who is finally ready for a break, God says, "Why don't you go on without me and I'll just stay home?" God decides to send the people forward without God's presence because of their stubbornness. God wants to send an angel to serve as an advance army to fight against the opposition. Though reluctantly, God decides not to go because the people's stubbornness will likely result in their death. They grieve this announcement. Stripping their ornaments, they ritually mourn God's decision. Withdrawal or withholding of God's presence from them is something to mourn and grieve. The people now believe that God might respond to their cries. They desperately want God to accompany them on this journey.

GOD'S FRIEND INTERVENES (33:7-23)

With God's open acknowledgment of God's continued frustration with the people, and the danger of going with God in this condition, Exodus reveals another layer to the relationship between Moses and God. Exodus gives important background to the relationship between God and God's chosen leader. This sometimes contentious outer relationship is not the full picture. Moses and God routinely meet face to face, not as leader and follower but as friend to friend. Outside the camp, Moses has a tent meeting with God, and God signifies God's approval and presence through the pillar of cloud (33:11).

Their relationship serves as background for the next transition. Using a play on the phrase "face to face," Moses demonstrates that God has seen him and the people, and they have now seen God's activity and work. Without God's presence leading them, there is no mission and certainly no people. Moses refuses to move forward without his friend's presence. His intervention echoes much of what he said to God before returning to Egypt. "How will they know who sent me?" God responded, "Tell them I AM THAT I AM has sent you" (Exod 3:13-14). God knows Moses' name; now Moses wants to know how God is going to be known (33:17). The people know God's presence through the pillar of cloud and fire, and Moses knows God's name. Moses also reminds God again that God created this "nation" and that these people are not a people without God's presence. God's presence makes Israel a viable group. Without it, they return back to the "no people" they once were under the Egyptians.

In response to the people's mourning and Moses' intercession, God gives Moses everything he asks for. God recommits to being presence with the people. God proclaims God's name before them and shows them grace and mercy (33:19-23). But God withholds from Moses the privilege of a face-to-face relationship from this point on. No longer willing to have the intimate meeting in the tent, God prepares Moses for a change in their relationship. Moses will be able to see God's back side as God's glory passes by but will no longer see God's face.

Renewing the Treaty (34:1-35)

Moses and most of the people survive the greatest threat to the journey—themselves. God plans to withdraw God's presence. Because of Moses' intercession, God changes his mind and commits to go with them so that they can maintain their identity. In the process, we learn the difficulties of leading a community and the challenges of following a mysterious, jealous God. To ratify the agreement, God invites Moses to the top of the mountain for forty days of fasting, praying, and recommitment. God reveals the core of God's character and laws that will guide the people forward through the next part of the journey.

CHARACTER REVEALED (34:1-9)

God invites Moses to meet on the mountain, where God cuts two new tablets so that God may write a new covenant treaty with the people. God proclaims God's name, then answers the question Moses asked in Exodus 6 and now asks again in Exodus 33: "Who are you?" These descriptions are the full definition of what "I AM THAT I AM" means. God reveals the core of God's character in psalm-like fashion. These words form the basis for our relationship with God in community today.

Merciful—the Hebrew word comes from the same root as the word for a mother's womb. The language suggests that God cares for and defends the people like a mother does for a child. Like a mama bear protecting her cubs from outside forces and one that fiercely enforces protective rules on her child, God is merciful toward God's children.

Gracious—God has granted the people unmerited favor. God's graciousness means that the gift of calling them out of Egypt could not have been earned. The gift of law and direction is given to the people because of God's character, not from a sense of merit or fidelity. God doesn't give them the law because they followed God. God grants them God's presence because of who God is.

Slow to anger—The word in Hebrew literally means "long-nosed." In this sense, God demonstrates that despite the initial impression of fury, God allows himself to cool off. That is, as the Hebrew suggests, the heat of God's nostrils has now cooled.

Abounding in steadfast love—God's love puts up with a lot of misbehavior.

Faithfulness—The Hebrew word is *hesed*, continual fidelity and loving-kindness toward the people.

Forgiving—The Hebrew root here comes from the root for lifting the burden. So just as God is continually loving to the thousandth generation, God is now willing to lift the burden of sin on the people

The qualities of God's character do not, however, excuse the behavior of the people or prevent the natural consequences of wrongdoing. God reiterates what God said earlier in Exodus. For now, future generations will feel the effects of their ancestors' sin. God's presence comes with a paradox. God forgives and punishes. But this promise is enough to keep God's presence with the people and plan for a hope and a future open to new possibilities. Remember: this is a God who is willing to change God's mind, and eventually God will do just that in Ezekiel (Ezek 18:1-9).

Overcome by the awe of the moment and in dedication to God, Moses prostrates himself (34:8). He prays to a God who demonstrates sovereign generosity toward Moses and the people. He prays again for the Lord to go with the people despite their stubbornness. Because they are so stiff-necked, Moses knows that God's presence is the only thing that will save them.

COVENANT RENEWED (34:10-28)

God announces the revised focus of the post-calf treaty. Now that he's seen how his people operate, God offers seven steps to keep the people alive and maintain God's presence among them.

1. Performative acts of power (vv. 10-11). God will show other people who God is throughout the nations. These activities will bear witness to God's character and remind the people of God's presence with them.

2. Protection against those who oppose God's people (vv. 11-16). Instead of sending an angel to drive out enemies, God will fight for the people. Notice that the people do not require a standing army or any army at all. God's presence provides the protection they will need. Their job is to remain loyal and faithful to God. They will not need peace treaties with these people because any treaty with locals will only contaminate the tribes and create renewed disloyalty, much as they experienced with the calf. At this point in the journey, they are not to share table fellowship or intermarry with other people.

3. Prohibition of fashioning cast idols (34:17). For obvious reasons, because of the golden calf, building idols never works.

4. Continuation of the New Year's Day/Passover festival (34:18). God wants them to continually recall the Passover deliverance.

5. Dedication of the firstborn, from people to flocks (34:19). God installs the redemption pattern of "buying back/redeeming" the firstborn male with a lamb, a pair of pigeons, or turtledoves. This pattern will continue until the temple in Jerusalem falls (Lev 12:1-8; Luke 2:23).

6. Continuation of Sabbath observance and three festivals each year (34:21-25). The people observe three festivals: weeks, wheat harvest, and ingathering.

7. Continuation of giving generously from the best of the produce (34:26). The covenant requires the people to give the best of everything to God.

After forty days in God's presence, Moses brings the tablets down from the mountain shining and transformed. Aaron, who has been blamed for the insurrection, still maintains his role among the people. Moses, however, has changed. Once the murderer, then the leader of God's people, and then the friend of God, now he has met face to face with the Lord and been transformed into a new kind of messenger of God's glory.

God's presence in Exodus can be described as one thing—glory. Just as God reveals himself in 24:16 and will eventually inhabit the tabernacle, so God revealed God's glory to Moses on the mountain, resulting in Moses' shining face. God's glory is inspiring, authoritative, dangerous, and wonderful. God's glory saves, leads, communicates, and fellowships.

This passage is the only time we learn that Moses adds a veil over his face when he speaks to the people, but this statement becomes an important interpretive symbol in 2 Corinthians 3:12-15. Paul mentions the veil to explain how Jews in Corinth who had not yet converted to following Jesus as Lord were functioning like Israelites in the wilderness. Paul was not demonstrating that Christianity is a superior religion to that of the ancient Israelites of the Exodus. Paul shows how this story from ancient Israelite tradition anticipates the work that Jesus does.

By studying Exodus carefully, we see that Moses' veil is a sign of God's presence among the people and a demonstration of the overwhelming majesty of God in their midst. The veil reveals how God's glory is the ultimate expression of God's love for them and shows the transforming power that God's glory has had on the people and even on God himself. God has changed the dynamics of the relationship with God's people in order to stay with them. A veil over Moses' face is only symbolic of this holy experience of renewal.

A Glorious Presence

People who learn to work together go through natural stages with each other—gathering, storming, norming, performing.[2] The Israelites have just been gathering and learning about who they are and who God is. God learns about what kind of people God has and decides whether God wants to be associated with them. Moses changes and grows into a reluctant leader. God decides for the community that the best way to be associated with them and for others to know that God is with them is not through static figures but through a mobile worship center designed for people to offer sacrifices and conduct their worship in God's presence. But part of the process of community identification and formation is waiting. The people, who have only known static figures, decide to implore their priest Aaron to make a bull so that they can worship God.

After the gathering stage, the people are storming. They commit two sins, both of which are intertwined. They commit idolatry and apostasy. They fashion an idol out of the jewelry they made, and in doing so they commit apostasy, abandoning the God they were following.

But God also wants to abandon the people God has committed to. God wants to be "left alone." He argues with Moses, and Moses intercedes on behalf of the people. Even despite these intercessions, and despite Moses' attempts to atone for their sin, God still cleanses people from the community in order to purify the whole group for the journey ahead. If God is going to be associated with these people, they need to be holy.

We learn a lot about the God who leads us, dwells with us, and renews God's creation with us over a Noah-like forty days and forty nights. But we can't have the full picture of the relationship with God until we've seen the apostasy. We also can't have a building project without sabotage and revolt. Just ask Nehemiah, the government worker sent to rebuild the city of Jerusalem after the Babylonians destroyed in 586 BCE, or anyone else who has tried to erect a religious structure.

Anyone venturing into church leadership or parenting should study this passage for what it reveals about the nature of leadership and the relationship we have with God. People are messy, and God is complex. Out of God's glorious character, God gets angry in ways that parents do toward their children and toward each other. God wants to be left alone and responds openly to prayerful argumentation. God is feared and faithfully followed. It's no wonder that in the end, Moses can only see the back side of God. Just a glimpse is enough to reveal that God's glory is shrouded in mystery.

If that's case with God, what can we learn about ourselves and the people under our care? Authentic leadership and life in a congregation can be studied through the reality of betrayal and treachery. Exodus tells us to expect it and learn from it; a relationship with God mirrors life in community. Following God begins out of wilderness apostasy. Just as Jonah went through the belly of a fish, there is no path to the promised land without an experience like the golden calf.

Nothing should surprise us in family dynamics. As we learn from Exodus, generations carry sin and blessings for years into the future. We can't blame ourselves for our grandchildren's mistakes, and our grandchildren can't blame us for their mistakes. But we can learn from each other. Generational systems teach us that the best way to approach problems and failures—even our own—is fidelity to God and courage to trust in God's glorious presence. At the core, God is merciful, gracious, compassionate, and forgiving. God is going before us to deal with enemies. Our job is to keep Sabbath, celebrate God's presence, and train future generations about God's awesome glory. When apostasy happens, we will be ready for the next challenge along the journey and the realization that God doesn't abandon us when we forsake God; God is more willing to stay with us now that we know who God is and who we are.

Leaders change their minds, and so does God. Our view of God's character as well as God's views of us change along the way. In the process, we are transformed as God's people, and God uses us in ways that we did not expect.

Stubbornness is not a sign of sin; it's a sign of presence. God chooses to go with the people because God knows how stubborn they are. Stubbornness can be a lethal strength and can result in the people's death. So God stays, and we keep marching on.

1. This study suggests that the people are not guilty of turning away from God but instead guilty of worshiping God the wrong way. What objects that we use for the worship of God today might become a barrier between us and God?

_____

_____

_____

_____

_____

2. God's statement "let me alone" can be interpreted in a number of ways. Practice saying the phrase in different tones of voice. How does vocal inflection change your sense of the words? Compare this statement to Exodus 33:1-6, when God wants the people to go on without him. How would you read this passage aloud?

_____

_____

_____

_____

_____

3. Moses changes as a leader in these chapters. How have you changed over the years as a result of a child's or someone else's mutiny? How did you and your family or organization grow?

_____

_____

_____

_____

_____

Notes

1. Leon F. Seltzer, "The Anger Thermostat: What's the Temperature of Your Upset?" in *Psychology Today*. Accessed June 9, 2020, psychologytoday.com/us/blog/evolution-the-self/201401/the-anger-thermostat-whats-the-temperature-your-upset.

2. Bruce Tuckman, "Developmental Sequence in Small Groups," *Psychological Bulletin* 63 (1965): 384–99.

The Presence of God:
Where Does God Dwell?

Exodus 35:1–40:38

When my wife, Kelly, was nominated to be president of the parent-teacher organization (PTO) at our son's elementary school, she discovered that there was money set aside for a still-incomplete project. For several years, parents had given money for a walking trail to circle the playground. The school always had other projects that were more important, and there was not enough money to begin construction. The school principal asked for additional money to start new initiatives, but there was not enough money to finish the old walking trail project. The volunteers were frustrated that their projects were never finished, and the PTO resorted to fundraisers that diverted them from their mission of helping students and children.

I assumed that when Kelly was president, she would use her year at the helm to finish the walking trail. She had even bigger plans. She and a team of moms decided they needed to finish the old project first in order to inspire the parents to contribute more. In the spring, when she was president-elect, they organized committees to finish the trail.

The moms organized people into teams, held meetings house to house to explain the need, and encouraged people to finish the job. Construction began on the trail that summer while the students were out of school. By the time they held the next fundraiser, people were excited about contributing because the school used the money that had been given for the intended cause. Instead of repeating the same fundraisers, the PTO changed the way they operated, and the school was renewed.

In a similar way, the Israelites had made progress toward a tabernacle. The cause for the delay was not the result of poor planning but their own destructive behavior. While waiting for Moses to finish receiving instructions, they turned away from God. Like any other leader who has attempted to guide a loosely structured group through a task, we can at least sympathize with the frustrated Moses. Every church can testify to a time when they thought they were doing the right thing in calling a pastor, building a building, or moving forward with a new ministry plan—only to see the plans change midstream. With the opportunity to restart, the Israelites needed not only a plan for construction but also a new way of going about being God's people. They certainly did not want to go back to Egypt; instead, they wanted to move forward together the way God wanted them to, with a healthy dose of the spirit of God.

Sometimes a job needs to be completed in order for the next project to be revealed. In the case of the Israelites, the tabernacle needs to be finished in the right way with the right resources. God reset the clock to recreate the people. He brings them back to the festival of Passover to begin construction and turned to Bezalel and several women who wanted to finish the job. God also positions Moses in the role where he started—as the one who could bless the work that others did. With Moses taking on a different role as a leader, the time finally comes to design and construct the desert worship center and to welcome the God of the cloud into their midst. We learn to reorganize our lives around Sabbath, delegate the work to the people, and use the gifts God has already entrusted to the community.

Sabbath Assembly (35:1-3)

At each stage of Israel's journey—from Egypt to the sea to the wilderness and finally to the tabernacle—preparation is the process. Obedience is the journey. Like them, we don't journey in order to learn what God wants. We obey, and God journeys with us and reveals along the way what God wants. The goal for the Israelites is God's presence in their midst—not a place with territory and boundaries. The purpose of the journey in the wilderness is to form them to be the people who could erect a tabernacle for God's presence to dwell among them.

As we've learned, the ideas for designing a mobile tent of meeting/tabernacle do not always match up with reality. In the midst of design, the people abandon their loyalty to God. They seek what is expedient rather than wait for the gift from God. God plans for mandated and voluntary gifts; but in reality, people under the leadership of Aaron offer the wrong gift at the wrong time.

Now, with a reconstituted people, they have a chance to implement what God designs. How often do we say after a project is complete, "I wish we would have done this the first time; it would have been much less expensive"? The Israelites finish the building of the tabernacle with virtually the same instructions that they received before their apostasy. But this time their priorities are in a different order; they follow the pattern of recreation as their people are re-created. Then they also utilize different people in the construction—a sign of God's presence, a mobile God who moves with his people through the wilderness.

The first step to build the tabernacle is not a step at all. It's a day marked as New Year's Day, not to be confused with our own January 1. This day marks the dawn of a new era for Israel and is closely associated with the days of creation. Construction begins on the Sabbath Day and ends on New Year's Day. Just as the Sabbath ended creation and marked the time when God ceased from God's labors, so the people "begin" their re-creation out of the "palace in time" called the Sabbath. They cannot be a people who worship Yahweh without marking the Sabbath. Their day of rest is just as significant to the reconstituted people as the dietary and relationship laws they follow. Fidelity to God is tantamount to resting one day each week. The assembly (a word similar to *ecclesia* or "called-out ones") joins together at the tabernacle on the Sabbath, and Sabbath indicates the start of a new beginning for the people.

Spiritual Empowerment (35:4–36:7)

Following the Sabbath assembly, another offering is taken. Earlier, before the design process began, God instructed Moses to receive an offering from those "whose hearts prompt them to give" (25:2). Now, when the offering is taken, people share their talent and treasure (35:22). The act of generosity is a holistic process that involves their work and their wealth. This time, there are three unique features.

1. People offer talent and treasure. Both participate equally in the offering, and there is no distinction between finances and merchandise. For example, "women whose hearts moved them to use their skill spun goats' hair" (35:26). The significance of these unnamed women cannot be overstated. In the first offering for the tabernacle before the calf, the men brought nice things to give but left out a critical part. There were no women mentioned in the story (Exod 25:1-9). Obviously, those men had no clue how to run the world. So this time around, instead of limiting giving to a select group of people (or one big-dollar donor), everyone has a chance to give. Interestingly, the language used in the text suggests that the women give out of their dowries from their weddings.[1] Because most received dowries from their fathers before they were married to their husbands, they gave what would be considered their only savings, an amount intended for their care if their husbands died. By giving their dowries to God, these women showed tremendous faith that God would honor the gift and provide for their future if required.

So the work is not limited just to the wealthy or the heavy hitters or to the naming opportunities; *everyone*, from those who stitched clothes to those who cut stone, had an equal part in the sacrifice to God. One of the first offerings that has ever been given is also one of the only examples where the preacher said, "Stop giving." The people brought too much.

These gifts illustrate the role that everyone plays in the construction of the tabernacle and the seamless connection among divine empowerment, personal talents, and skills used to earn an income. Money and skills are equally interwoven. Each artisan is responsible for different portions of the offering based on their spirit-empowered vocation. God calls and assembles the congregation, then empowers them with skills that are used for work, wealth, wisdom, and witness. Later, when the tabernacle is constructed, unnamed women serve at the entrance to the tent of meeting (38:8). What they give to and how they serve are linked.

2. God calls artisans and architects. Closely connected to the unique form of offering are the people who design and construct the tabernacle. God calls people and fills them with skills, knowledge, and wisdom. Bezalel emerges as an example of one who has the vocation of architect. We first meet Bezalel and his team in the design phase (31:1-11), when the story emphasizes the priestly role of Aaron and his family. Bezalel is the first person recorded in Scripture on whom the Spirit of God falls. He's an architect, contractor, and brick mason for the tabernacle. He has a handy assistant named Oholiab, and the two of them take the burden off Moses and everyone else. The Spirit of God ordains the natural wisdom, discernment, and talents of the people. Bezalel has three significant qualities. He's wise—he can connect rules to relationships and knows how to apply the rules of construction to what the people need. He has discernment—he knows when to keep his mouth shut and when to open it. And he has talent—he can do this job and has an eye for design.

This is why the tabernacle offering is so critical. God's movement does not happen only when the glory of God dwells among the people in chapter 40. God's work happens in the design and offering phase too. The Celts describe the place where God's presence seems to touch earth as a "thin place."[2] There is no thin place of worship unless the movement of God has been experienced in the planning, in the design, and in the discernment.

The construction phase now focuses on the vocation of architects and builders who represent the gifts that are deployed by the assembly for God's purpose in the wilderness. Construction is an apprenticeship experience. And as Bezalel and Oholiab construct the tabernacle, they teach others to do the same.

3. God empowers them with the gifts and skills to carry out the work. God's Spirit falls on the people, endows them with their talents, gives them the capacity to work, and allows them to receive material benefit from their skills. Their offerings are linked to their talents. God uses the offerings to identify people who have skills and talents for the construction phase. They give what they normally do. For example, those who have skills in textiles offer gifts that will go into the making of the curtains. For pilgrim people like these Israelites, there is no separation between money, work, charity, and church. They are all holistically interwoven together through their lives.

4. The offering is more than anyone could have expected. So much is given that Moses has to stop the offering "For what they had already brought was more than enough to do all the work" (36:7).

Sacred Space (36:8–38:31)

The "tabernacle of the covenant" serves four purposes: it is a location where God touches earth, a place where people can offer their sacrifices to God and know that God receives them, a reminder to the people that God has made a peace treaty with them to lead them, and a witness to other people of Israel's God. They have a God who is present with them and allows them to worship God while traveling. The construction begins with a sacred time and moves to a reality of people on the move. Because of the functional nature of the tabernacle, the construction phase needs to follow a similar pattern. Prior to the golden calf incident, God had a formula. Now there is a function. Construction differs from design in the order it takes place as well as in the people involved.

Function follows form this time. In the design phase, the writer listed the objects for the tabernacle presumably in the priority of their sacred functions:

1. Ark (25:10-22)
2. Table (25:23-30)
3. Lampstand (25:31-40)
4. Curtains (26:7-14)
5. Altar (27:1-19)

In the construction phase, the writer focuses on the logical order for using God's tabernacle. First build the enclosure, and then place the objects inside.

1. Curtains (36:8-35)
2. Ark (37:1-9)
3. Table (37:10-16)
4. Lampstand (37:17-24)
5. Altar (37:25-28)

Two other notable differences occur in the building process. First, as mentioned in the previous section, women play a significant role at the entrance of the tent of meeting. Just as they have donated their services and textiles, they also contribute mirrors and serve at the entrance. Women are involved at the beginning of the exodus story through the five women who saved Moses' life as well as in the concluding work of worship.

Second, the construction phase highlights the amassed treasure of metals used to construct the furnishings and reprises the character of Ithamar (6:23; 28:1; see chapter 5 above). He serves as a project manager, accounting for the metals used for construction. We can only speculate about the origins of these metals. This particular list was not included in the design. It is obvious, though, that the people are not poor pilgrims. God supplies them with abundant resources for worshiping God (38:21-31). Just as the writer of Revelation highlights the valuable metals used in prophetic worship spaces, so God's earthly worship space reflects the future temple (Rev 21:15-21). The people also account for the resources. They are good stewards of what God has provided.

Satisfied Leader (39:1-43)

In the previous design of the tabernacle (Exod 28:1–31:10), Aaron figured prominently around the theme of holy objects, both sacred and profane. Now the focus is on getting the work done so that the people can have a place for God to dwell. The work begins in rest and ends in re-creation. Aaron isn't nearly as prominent now. Moses is.

A theme is repeated seven times in Exodus 39: "As the LORD commanded Moses" (vv. 1, 5, 7, 21, 26, 29, 31); this theme also continues in chapter 40. Moses satisfies God's expectations by obeying him and leaving the work of construction and implementation to the people the Spirit has empowered. With the tabernacle completed and the materials accounted for, the last step before the arrival of God's presence is to finish the garments. In this chapter, attention returns to Moses as priestly leader, not Aaron. In the design phase before the apostasy, Aaron and his sons figured prominently. Now, even as a flawed leader, Moses resumes his place in the story. The vestments for the priesthood are largely the same as Aaron wore prior to the apostasy, but the person for whom they are designed is barely mentioned. Aaron and his sons are only mentioned once (39:27). In this section, the emphasis falls on how Moses obediently fulfills his role as the priestly leader of the people and accomplishes what he was sent to do: lead them out of slavery so that they can worship God alone.

In order to finish the work (39:32-33), the people symbolically bring the tabernacle to Moses (39:33). He examines the work and blesses them. In the end, Moses stays out of the construction phases so that God can use the people that God has anointed and gifted to do their work well. Just as God finishes the work of creation, now the community finishes and completes the work finalized by Moses. Now the community rests and gives offerings, and their leader finalizes the construction.

The people bring the work to conclusion by delivering their work to their leader, and the leader blesses the work. In this way, Moses illustrates another way that a community is re-created and ready to rest. God creates us, and we build a microcosm/intersection of a mobile God and people on the move.

Settled Cloud (40:1-38)

The final stage of the construction of God's tabernacle begins with the new year. Tent accompanies time. Just as the Israelite new year is marked by the festival of Passover, so it is now signified with a place for God's presence to dwell. God has guided them as a cloud by day and a pillar of fire by night out of Egypt and to Sinai. Now God's guiding presence leads them to a mobile dwelling place—not a static destination. Instead of taking them to a final destiny, the last instructions indicate the kind of mission the people embody: Their mission in Exodus is not to try to arrive in the promised land. Their mission is to live as God's people, doing what the Lord commands. They are to be focused on serving God's presence all the time—not just whenever they arrive in the land. In so doing, they have a mission in time all the time.

Moses follows God's instructions again and completes the work on the tabernacle that God began at creation in Genesis, continued through Moses' deliverance out of the Nile, and fulfills here in the wilderness. Through setting, anointing, washing, and erecting, Moses "finishes the work" (Exod 40:33b) that the gifted artisans, architects, and textile workers constructed. Moses and Aaron return again as brothers to wash their hands and feet before they enter the tent of meeting (40:31-32). The word "finish" is *kalal* in Hebrew, the same word used for God's work to finish creation.

God arrives and plans to continue leading the people on in a cloud. Just as God appeared in a cloud at certain points in Exodus and will again appear at the Mount of Transfiguration (Matt 17:1-8), so now God's presence is still signified by the divine. We know that God's presence dwells with us. John uses the same imagery when he describes what Jesus does in John 1:14. He "tabernacles" among us. God is mobile enough to keep guiding us forward. God initiates the process forward, and the people respond. The Hebrew phrase to describe this place literally means "Dwelling Place of the Tent of Meeting."

The one true God is both a mobile God and a God who dwells wherever people have assembled to do whatever God commands. God creates a people to reflect God's character. The congregation/church is both a tabernacle and a temple people, mobile pilgrims and a people placed on a rock (Heb 12:1-13; Matt 16:13-20; 1 Peter 2:9-12). God dwells wherever the people are rooted, and the people are on mission to follow the moving cloud wherever the cloud takes them. The emphasis is not on knowing when and where the cloud will lead them. They are to trust in the one who is behind the cloud and is also with them, dwelling in their midst. As God stays with them, so they trust in God's presence. In other words, God is not simply waiting for them in the transition; God is in the transition as well as in the next stage on the journey.

God's presence with the people is made possible because of God's initiative and the people's obedience. The tabernacle is portable but not permanent. God's presence is permanent *and* portable. The question for the people is whether they are willing to erect the tabernacle as a sign of obedience and public commitment to Yahweh, live by God's commands, and allow God's presence to fill their lives and direct their movements. Every time God moves, people have a chance to recommit and reconnect to following God. The work of setting up and tearing down is an ongoing activity that shows our fidelity to Yahweh's presence, a sign that we want Yahweh to come, and an acknowledgment that we are dependent on a God who delivers, dwells, and decides where to take us next. Wherever God is, we are invited to follow. Wherever we are, God is seeking us out to deliver us and to invite us to dwell with him.

For the Israelites, that obedience comes with a certain set of liturgies and preparations with priests and functions, similar to the practices of other ancient peoples. But these are also part of the obedience of God's people. Instead of an altar at various locations at Bethel, the altar for God is portable because the people are on the move, and so is their God. Wherever the people obey and erect the shrine, God dwells.

Leaders and Followers for a Church Worshiping in the Wilderness

Like the Israelites, churches today often minister to people through a wilderness journey: pastoral transitions, declining attendance, emerging mission and ministry, and restructures of church as we know it today. What emerges from the story of Exodus is that wilderness is not a punishment; wilderness is the place where God leads the people so that God can inhabit the wilderness with them. God needs to get them out of Egypt and delay occupation of the new territory to remind the people why God wanted to be with them in the first place—so they could worship God, so God could dwell with them, and so they would follow if God decided to keep moving.

The most important journey that the church takes is one the leaders make. Moses transforms his image of leadership from privileged mentor to victim to shepherd to frustrated guide and, finally, to obedient recipient. Moses shares his spiritual direction with others. This is true charismatic leadership as opposed to celebrity leadership. Moses leads by giving his power away and enlarging others who have a role. These others prophesy and interpret. They are willing to hear God's voice and speak what they hear to the people. The real test of leadership in the spirit-led community is whether the leader will help the group arrive at a decision in a way that helps the people believe it was their idea all along. This kind of charismatic leader understands a person's limits and necessarily wants to share the ideas, energy, credit, and resources with others. Spiritual direction is shared direction. It's learning to understand that the cloud over my head is a sign of God's presence rather than God's punishment. The only way to know is through the movement of the spirit, which is sometimes surprising, sometimes satisfying, and sometimes disturbing.

Because Moses is able to surrender his need to be involved in everything, God has room to reconstitute the people and give them a new imagination for freedom and generosity. Freedom does not mean liberation from the oppressor or occupation of a new land. As David Bentley Hart notes,

> We become free in the same way a sculptor liberates a sculpture from marble. This means we are free not merely because we can choose, but only when we have chosen well. For to choose poorly through folly or malice, in a way that thwarts our nature and distorts our proper form, is to enslave ourselves to the transitory, the irrational, the purposeless, the subhuman.[3]

Hart suggests that God has liberated the people from Egypt in the way the sculptor reveals the sculpture inside the marble. Out of the confining space of Egypt, now the people are free to be present with the God who always wanted to be present with them.[4]

In response, the people offer abundant resources that provide more than what is needed for the project. A different kind of congregation/assembly and a different kind of leadership is required for these times, but these are also the times when the people of Exodus find themselves. Consider the area of generosity.

God focuses our attention away from routine and instead onto abilities. A spiritual gifts "test" becomes a connection point between gift, talent, and tithe. Generosity begins when we ask a new set of questions. For example, consider how Exodus reshapes our imagination around generosity. Most churches measure success through the offering plate, and many discuss tithing as the best way to raise resources for God's work. Exodus goes a step further by connecting gifts, talents, and tithes. Exodus asks new questions about how we can connect our work and our gifts to God's work. Where has God already called us uniquely in our vocation, and how can that be used in the construction of our assembly space? How can the gifts received from income be deployed generously for a portion of our work? We have seen each other work and recognize the connection between our work, giving, worshiping, and ministry. Our work is literally liturgy—a public work and offering to God.

This pattern can be illustrated this way: With a focus on God's presence at the center of the community (tabernacle), we use our time, talents, income, and trade. The Spirit integrates these resources together to reimagine the abundant generosity of God. By asking these questions, we can cause new streams of generosity to bubble forth. A public schoolteacher's work and vocation can be offered for the educational ministry of the church. A construction worker's skills can keep the facilities of the congregation functioning. A hospital chaplain's gift can help the caring ministry of the congregation. A talented seamstress can create blankets for new babies. When we use our talents to assist in ministry, God multiplies our spiritual and financial resources to provide a gathering place and ministry center to meet God.

1. Take a look at your work, school, or training. How can your church use your experience in service of the congregation? What untapped areas of expertise can be utilized?

_____

_____

_____

_____

_____

2. How can your source of income be used to as a channel of blessing in God's kingdom? How can you use the skills by which you earn a living as an avenue of generosity toward the church?

_____

_____

_____

_____

_____

3. How has your definition of leadership changed as you worked with people? How do leaders give their power away and allow the Spirit to move?

_____

_____

_____

_____

_____

4. How does God become present to you in the midst of any transition in life? How can you see the wilderness as a time of God's activity?

_____

_____

_____

_____

_____

5. How does Sabbath rest become a witness for your church? How can you rearrange your schedule to make room for God to do his work of re-creation?

_____

_____

_____

_____

_____

Notes

1. John Durham, *Exodus*, Word Biblical Commentary 3 (Waco: Word Books, 1987), 477.

2. Tracy Balzar, *An Evangelical Journey into Celtic Christianity* (Abilene: Leafwood Publishers, 2007), 23–24.

3. David Bentley Hart, *Atheist Delusions: The Christian Revolution and Its Fashionable Enemies* (New Haven: Yale University Press, 2010), 25.

4. Hart, *Atheist Delusions*, 25.

Bibliography

Brooks, David. "The Power of Posterity." *New York Times.* July 27, 2009. nytimes.com/2009/07/28/opinion/28brooks.html.

Brueggemann, Walter. "Antidote to Amnesia." In *Reclaiming the Imagination: The Exodus as Paradigmatic for Preaching,* edited by David Fleer and David Bland, 7–25. Nashville: Chalice Press, 2009.

Brueggemann, Walter. "Exodus." In *General Articles on the Bible, General Articles on the Old Testament, the Book of Genesis, the Book of Exodus, the Book of Leviticus.* Volume 1 of New Interpreter's Bible. Nashville: Abingdon, 1994.

Dawn, Marva. *Keeping the Sabbath Wholly: Ceasing, Resting, Embracing, Feasting.* Grand Rapids, MI: Eerdmans, 1989.

Durham, John. *Exodus.* Word Biblical Commentary 3. Waco, TX: Word Books, 1987.

Fretheim, Terence. *Exodus.* Interpretation. Louisville, KY: John Knox, 1991.

Frost, Robert. *The Road Not Taken, Birches, and Other Poems.* Claremont, CA: Coyote Canyon Press, 2010.

Hart, David Bentley. *Atheist Delusions: The Christian Revolution and Its Fashionable Enemies.* New Haven, CT: Yale University Press, 2010.

Heschel, Abraham, and Ilya Schor. *The Sabbath.* 3rd edition. New York: Farrar, Strauss, Giroux, 2005.

Howlett, John, ed. *Invictus: Selected Poems and Prose of W. E. Henley.* Portland, OR: Sussex Academic Press, 2018.

Kipling, Rudyard. *Kipling Poems.* Everyman's Library. New York: Alfred Knopf, 2007.

Long, Thomas. *Preaching from Memory to Hope.* Louisville, KY: Westminster John Knox Press, 2009.

Matthews, Victor. *Social World of Ancient Israel, 1250-587 BCE.* Peabody, MA: Hendrickson, 1993.

Meyers, Carol. *Exodus.* New Cambridge Bible Commentary. Cambridge: Cambridge University, 2005.

Peterson, Eugene. *Christ Plays in Ten Thousand Places: A Conversation in Spiritual Theology.* Grand Rapids, MI: Eerdmans, 2008.

Shiell, William D. "'I Will Give You a Mouth and Wisdom': Prudent Speech in Luke 21:15." *Review and Expositor* 112/4 (2015): 609–17.

Trueblood, Elton. *Foundations for Reconstruction.* Waco, TX: Word Books, 1972.